100
Years
of
Architecture

Published in 2016 by
Laurence King Publishing Ltd
361–373 City Road
London EC1V 1LR
United Kingdom
T +44 (0)20 7841 6900
F +44 (0)20 7841 6910
enquiries@laurenceking.com
www.laurenceking.com

A catalogue record for this
book is available from the
British Library.

ISBN
978-1-78067-823-8

Design
John Dowling / Mucho

Picture Research
Peter Kent

Printed in China

Front cover
Philips Pavilion, World Fair, Brussels, 1958
—
Le Corbusier (1887–1965) and Iannis Xenakis (1922–2001)
—
Designed to house a sound and light 'experience', the 'Electronic Poem' with music by Edgard Varèse, the concept of the Philips Pavilion came from Le Corbusier, but it was the musician–architect in his office, Xenakis, who designed the three-peaked tent with hyperbolic parabaloid curves, a tensile steel cable structure clad with concrete panels, on to whose interior surfaces a sequence of images was projected.

Frontispiece
Habitat 67, Montreal, 1967
—
Moshe Safdie (b.1938) See page 172

Back cover
Biosphere, Montreal, 1965–67
—
Richard Buckminster Fuller (1895–1983) See page 163

100 Years of Architecture

Alan Powers

Laurence King Publishing

Contents

—

Introduction 6–11
Further Reading 296
Index 296–302
Picture Credits 303–304
Acknowledgements 304

1

—

Memory, Modernity and Modernism

—

1890– 1914

—

12–37

2

—

Solidity and Scenography

—

1914– 1939

—

38–59

3

—

The New Reality

—

1914– 1932

—

60–85

4

—

The Lost Lands of Modernism

—

1929– 1950

—

86–103

5

—

Other Modern: Romanticism and Revision

—

1933– 1945

—

104–123

6

—

The New World

—

1945– 1970

—

124–159

7

—

New Fabrication and New Form

—

1920– 1975

—

160–181

8

—

Recovered Memory

—

1950– 2000

182–205

9

—

Landscape and Location

—

1965– 2014

—

206–229

10

—

High Tech and Low Tech

—

1975– 2014

—

230–249

11

—

Icons, Superstars and Global Brands

—

1980– 2014

—

250–273

12

—

Controlled Experience

—

1989– 2014

—

274–295

Introduction

Book cover design by László Moholy-Nagy (1895–1946): 'Building in France, Building in Iron, Building in Ferroconcrete', by Sigfried Giedion, 1928

—

Trained as an art historian under Heinrich Wölfflin, Giedion (1888–1968) played an important role in shaping the dominant narrative of the Modern movement as being derived from French experiments in iron construction and their spatial potential. Later in life, he turned to a more mystical approach, expressing doubts about the benefits of technology. This book, with its striking cover by a leading artist and Bauhaus teacher, was only translated into English for the first time in 1995.

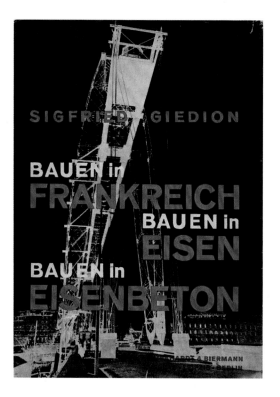

A hundred years of architecture at any point in history covers a lot of material, but for the period from 1914, it represents a crescendo of production linked to expanding population. Looked at as a totality, this body of work appears extremely varied, according to the developmental stages of the countries concerned, but it converges through this 100-year period towards a greater sameness in line with globalization.

The way that the history of this period has been written is rather different. Such a high degree of diversity is hard to contain in a single storyline, with the result that histories have been highly selective, and for a long time were usually based on a single interpretation – namely, that the twentieth century was unique because the long-hoped-for goal of a Modern architecture, not based on copying the past, had finally been achieved. For a time, the writing of history was inseparable from propaganda for this breakthrough. Historians from the 1920s, such as Sigfried Giedion, explained the character of this event, tracing it back to the mid-nineteenth century's development of new building techniques, combined with frustration over the superficial application of historic styles. The crucial issue was to sustain momentum and prevent backsliding. These writers picked out a line of development

'Modern Architecture: International Exhibition', Museum of Modern Art, New York, 1932, gallery installation
—
This exhibition, curated by Philip Johnson (1906–2005) with Henry-Russell Hitchcock (1903–87), fixed the idea that Modernism in architecture was primarily about a certain look. Their book, *The International Style*, 1932, linked to the exhibition, was widely distributed and, although its simplistic interpretation was soon rejected by both authors, the phrase itself and its adverse connotations of suppressed national character were too convenient to be forgotten. In the photo, we see the model of Le Corbusier's Villa Savoye taking pride of place.

represented by key buildings such as Le Corbusier's Villa Savoye near Paris, the Bauhaus building in Dessau, and the German Pavilion in Barcelona by Mies van der Rohe, all dating from the years between 1925 and 1930. These buildings featured prominently in the famous 1932 exhibition in New York that coined the description, the 'International Style'. These shining buildings (each of them rescued from near death, or in the Barcelona case, resurrected as a facsimile) carry a potent message of a utopian future after the destruction of World War I, before it was lost with the rise of Fascist dictators and the destruction of World War II. They have remained among the benchmarks for what Modern architecture means, with their smooth white surfaces, large windows and their convincing demonstration that space, rather than surface, mass or composition, had now become the essential architectural quality, and they are still among the sacred pilgrimage sites of the cult of Modernism.

These pioneers of Modern architecture learned from ships, aeroplanes and grain silos that beauty is the product of unmediated technical processes, and should not be a question of conscious style. At the same time, it was the potential of the new architecture to change society that was most important, through an overall control of urban and regional planning, bringing order to the chaos created by industrialization. This vision of harmony and perfection, with its controlling and dogmatic ethos, was compelling.

These ideas have retained a hold, but much has happened since. After 1930, Modernism took a more romantic and regionalist turn, led in some cases by the former apostles of scientific exactitude. The change did not mean a reversion to the pre-Modernist condition, but was still a significant modification, and it seems that underlying it was a shift in scientific focus from physics to biology, with a corresponding change in the imagery of architecture from straight lines and grids, executed without texture, towards curves, rough surfaces and a conscious reaching out to nature. At the same time, in reaction to totalitarianism, buildings worked harder to represent the inclusion of all people in a nurturing environment. Folk building traditions, always an underlying influence in Modernism, were more explicitly reinterpreted as a basis for new design.

Villa at Liseleje, Denmark, 1949–50
—
Ole Hagen (1913–84)
—
Overlooked or denigrated by many histories of Modernism, the softer, more romantic approach to design of the middle decades of the twentieth century is arguably more relevant to current concerns than the more famous 'icon' buildings, as demonstrated in the pairing of pictures on this page. This is not just a question of style, but related to the materials and performance of buildings – in both of these cases, the use of timber to make a sheltered porch, extending the lines of gently sloping roofs.

Dundon Passivhaus, Somerset, England, 2013
—
Prewett Bizley Architects (Robert Prewett, b.1970, and Graham Bizley, b.1969)
—
Graham Bizley's own house is a demonstration of the best standards for low energy use, combined with a model for rural housing derived from the broad shapes of agricultural buildings. The poor environmental performance of many 'classic' Modernist buildings means that they are no longer suitable models for emulation, even if they can be admired as works of art.

**Stadsteatern, Götaplatsen,
Gothenburg, Sweden, 1929–34**
—
Carl Bergsten (1879–1935)
—
The Swedish port city of
Gothenburg held a major exhibition
in 1923, and a new civic square
was planned for it in a classical
style. By 1934, most Swedish
architects had become Modernists,
and the concert hall by Nils Einar
Eriksson of 1931–35 that faces
Bergsten's theatre is recognized
as an exemplar. Not so the theatre,
which does not fit the 'Swedish
Grace' paradigm of polite classicism
either, since it uses Ionic columns
and other elements in a playful,
'incorrect' manner, evoking the age
of French Revolutionary architecture
(then being rediscovered as a
possible source for Modernism),
while breaking the rules as James
Stirling did in the 1980s.

**Royal Opera House extension,
Covent Garden, London, 1983–99**
—
**Dixon Jones BDP (Jeremy Dixon,
b.1939, and Edward Jones, b.1939),
painting by Carl Laubin (b.1947)**
—
The use of classical elements
in a modern building has
always been contentious among
professional insiders while seldom
worrying the people or (in the
English case) their princes. In the
Postmodernist period, Jeremy
Dixon designed housing and public
buildings in which context played
a major role. Among these was the
opportunity to restore the effect of
a long-lost corner of Inigo Jones's
Covent Garden Piazza (1630), with
covered arcades. This strategy
is comparable to Carl Bergsten's
inventive use of classicism to
create a sense of traditional civic
space 50 years earlier.

The 1930s and 1940s are often seen as a retreat from the high ideals of
Modernism and their purest formal expression – from what Alison and Peter
Smithson labelled, in an article of 1965, 'The Heroic Period of Modern Architecture'.
The greater pluralism of the mid-century was dismissed as compromise, and
consequently much of its production was ignored, but the selection here
deliberately increases the coverage of those difficult years. It is the buildings of
that time in brick or timber, not necessarily flat-roofed, that could be mistaken for
the products of the present, rather than the white cubes that came before them –
not an absolute proof of their value, perhaps, but an indication that they were
not, after all, simply a dead end on the road.

Caribbean Hut, as exhibited at the Crystal Palace, London, 1851
—
Gottfried Semper (1803–79)
—
In London as a political exile in the year of the Great Exhibition, the German theorist and architect Gottfried Semper was fascinated by a hut, built of bamboo with woven panels filling the frame. This accorded with his theory that weaving was the primal activity in architecture and all other forms of making. Semper's theory of cladding runs as a semi-submerged theme through Modernism.

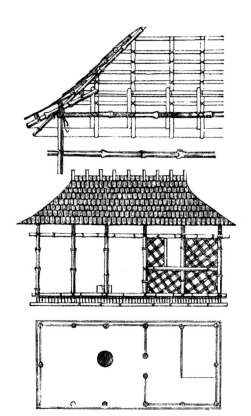

More challenging for many is to cross the stylistic line that separates the abstraction of Modern architecture from the overt representation of history and local tradition, but the history of twentieth-century architecture is not just the history of Modernism. This is where history has played a distorting role. Modernism began as a small encampment on one side of this line, and rather like the Christian Church, it suffered early persecution before emerging by the 1960s to suppress its rivals and take over the whole field. The role of Nazism and Stalinism in persecuting Modernism brought to the argument powerful but arguably extraneous proof of right and wrong, which led to a reverse persecution after 1945. The buildings of these regimes are barely represented here, but more space is given than in most books to the whole counter-current to Modernism in the twentieth century, extending before and after the totalitarian period. The chapters alternate as an antiphonal conversation between different sides, aiming to give each its due and defuse the polemical opposition between them.

In the 1980s, there was a many-faced revolt against the uniformity of architecture, represented as Postmodernism, but earlier deviations from the path had already pointed the way to a greater variety of ways of doing Modern architecture, so it could be argued that Postmodernism merely found itself a name, some slogans and some famous recruits to make something that was already present seem like a new movement.

While Modernism can claim to have begun within a few years before 1914, its intellectual roots and the development of its technical aspects go back much further. The historiography of Modernism itself contains many sub-cultures and conflicts, from which current architectural tribes draw their identity. Gottfried Semper, a mid-nineteenth-century German architect, proposed that rather than being primarily a matter of structure, architecture's origins were in weaving and textiles, so that the nature of the wall matters more than the bone structure of the framed support. This strand of thought was ignored for many years, but one of the most interesting examples of the dialogue between history and creativity is its return since the 1990s, encouraging a new interest in coloured materials and patterns, with a modest return to decorative surfaces, often generated by computer.

The history of Modernism was, for many years, distorted towards Western Europe and America, resulting from an unquestioned belief in their cultural supremacy that defined all canons of right and wrong, coupled with ignorance of what was happening in the rest of the world. Even with awareness it is difficult to redress the balance fully, but some attempt has been made.

Capturing the recent past is difficult, however one tries to do it. What follows is essentially a series of snapshots – not necessarily of buildings that will be inscribed in the histories to come as pioneers, but examples that show some of the diversity of practice around the world; humble local structures as well as grand showpieces. The combination of these opposite scales has always been present in Modernism, so that at no period does any single category give more than a fragementary picture of the whole.

It should perhaps be added that this book is based on the assumption that architecture means buildings. This might well be challenged, since unbuilt projects and speculative schemes for both real and unreal situations have contributed greatly to Modernism's identity in the artistic and intellectual sense. Other books do greater justice to this aspect, while here the main focus is on what was actually constructed and what has remained extant – often only owing to the efforts of conservationists to oppose demolition threats, seek legal protection and implement appropriate repairs.

Representing a building by a single image is equally open to challenge, for it tends to compound the problem that only photogenic buildings become accepted in the canon of history, when Modernism, in particular, was an attempt to go

Victoria and Albert Museum of Childhood, Bethnal Green, London, 1872, extended 2002–07

—

HRH Prince Albert (1819–61), extension by Caruso St John Architects (Adam Caruso, b.1962, and Peter St John, b.1959)

—

Gottfried Semper was involved in an earlier version of the design of an iron and glass structure known as the 'Brompton Boilers', which originally formed part of what is now the V&A Museum. It was moved to Bethnal Green, in East London, in 1872 and James William Wild added a new brick exterior with a rather Germanic style. When building a new frontage 130 years later, Caruso St John defied the Modernist prohibition on ornament by adding a Semperian wall decoration in coloured stone.

beyond the superficiality of the image in order to value less obvious aspects, such as the social contribution a building would make, or the unseen ingenuity of its structure or servicing. The photograph is especially problematic in that it can only go a little way towards representing space, the quality of architecture that Modernists felt was their special contribution to recovering from the weight of traditional building typology and surfaces loaded with ornament at the end of the nineteenth century. For the real experience of space, there is no substitute for visiting these buildings and getting to know them, inside and out.

1

Memory, Modernity and Modernism

1890 – 1914

Sant'Elia's drawings were exhibited in 1914, in connection with Italy's Futurist movement. They demonstrate the strand in Modernism that fed into and out of avant-garde movements in painting and sculpture. His vision of houses served by external elevators, standing astride railway tracks, epitomizes the Futurist ideal of dynamism and danger in extreme reaction to Italy's obsession with history. Forgotten for many years, these drawings inspired architects in the 1960s and beyond.

While the European war of 1914–18 marked major changes in politics and culture, the story of architectural change had an earlier beginning, around 1890. The intellectual and theoretical roots go back further still, with the idea that aesthetics in architecture should march in step with technology, while acting as the servant of society and, at times, as its leader. Industrial and engineering structures, railway bridges of iron and stone, or the enormous greenhouse that was the Crystal Palace in London in 1851, showed how unity of form, construction and symbolic imagery might work together, but only when the economics of construction began to be affected by reinforced concrete and affordable steel around 1890 did the greater change begin.

In the quarter-century before 1914, everyday life was transformed by telephones, electric light and motor cars. Movements in art and ideas accelerated – Cézanne, Freud, Einstein and Bohr; women and workers fought for basic rights and freedoms. Where was architecture's equivalent change?

It has often been assumed that the burden architecture had to free itself from was history, in the form of memories of older styles whose grammar and vocabulary contradicted the mechanized methods of modernity, so that Modernism could emerge as a new aesthetic of pure form, shaped by the logic of engineering and machine production of components. In Art Nouveau and its cognate forms, something different occurred – cultural memory, especially in nationalist form, mingled with the curves of nature to create a new decorative art freighted with meaning. As the *fin de siècle* mists began to clear, Frank Lloyd Wright's houses and other buildings around Chicago showed how the historic forms could be stretched, broken open and rearranged in a coherent and transmittable aesthetic that gave the third dimension of space an unprecedented clarity and excitement. From here, according to most standard accounts, the line of the future extended, with Gropius and Meyer's Fagus Factory of 1911 the first signpost on the route.

In recognizing this achievement, much of the rest of what was going on prior to 1914 has been demoted, if not deleted from the record. Among Wright's contemporaries in Europe was the generation that gave birth to other interwoven strands of Modernism. Perret, Behrens, Berlage and Wagner were all figures of enormous stature and influence as theorists and teachers, and, in the case of the last two, as city planners. All four men were involved in training architects, whether in academies or in their own offices, and in shaping the character of national styles in their respective countries for several generations to come. They straddled the academic establishment and the new worlds of art and expression. Each can be associated with certain materials – Perret with reinforced concrete, Behrens with steel, Berlage with brick, and Wagner with the use of decorative claddings that altered the relationship between surface and structure.

The period was, of course, much richer and more varied than this, and there were many other ways for architects to reconcile technical modernity with the legitimate claims of memory, leaving space for context and meaning while satisfying the Modernist aims of serving society.

**Glasgow School of Art,
1897–99, 1907–09**

—

**Charles Rennie Mackintosh
(1868–1928)**

—

The need for large studio windows
began the process of abstraction
that Mackintosh pursued in the
first phase of the School of Art. The
building draws on late Victorian
eclectic compositions, but turns
them in new directions. Ten years
later, when he completed his
building, Mackintosh had become
a European celebrity, but in
Glasgow his style was considered
old-fashioned. The library wing,
destroyed internally by fire in 2014,
exaggerates the sense of height.

**Crypt of the Colònia Güell
Chapel, San Coloma de Cervelló,
Barcelona, 1908–14**

—

Antoni Gaudí (1852–1926)

—

Gaudí was one of a group of
architects who transformed the
regional Gothic Revival of Catalonia
into a branch of the international
Art Nouveau movement. His patron,
Eusebio Güell, created a workers'
settlement whose unfinished chapel
stretched Gaudí's design method,
which involved catenary curves
modelled with hanging wires to
achieve forms analogous to nature.
Tiles, basalt and bricks, with grilles
made from scrap iron, contributed
to the phantasmagoric effect.

14

Amsterdam Stock Exchange, 1898–1903

—

Hendrik Petrus Berlage (1856–1934)

—

In his greatest project, prominently sited close to Amsterdam Central Station, Berlage realized 'the principle of good honest construction' based on the ideas of Semper and Viollet-le-Duc. All the elements are physically interlocked in the brick and stone walls of the Stock Exchange, where the supports for the cast iron roof are corbelled out from the brick wall 'naked ... in all its simple beauty'.

Austrian Postal Savings Bank, Vienna, 1904–6, 1910–12

—

Otto Wagner (1841–1918)

—

In the last years of the Habsburg Empire, Otto Wagner was the leading Viennese architect, city planner and teacher. The Savings Bank, a Catholic response to the conventional banks for the 'little man', simplifies a classical composition, suggesting Ruskin's 'confessed encrustation' of the wall with marble panels held by rivets, with countersunk aluminium heads – a metal still new to building – from which the sculptures on the roofline were also made.

**Unity Temple, Oak Park, Illinois,
1905–8**
—
Frank Lloyd Wright (1867–1959)
—
'I confess to a love for a clean arris;
the cube I find comforting.' Wright
told an older architect around the
time that he designed Unity Temple
in the Chicago suburb where his
career was launched. The concrete
structure encouraged repetition,
square in plan and subdivided by
its glazed grid roof, designed to
be seen as one enters at the corner.
Wright's influence spread to Europe
through the publication of this and
other designs.

American Bar, Kärntner Durchgang, Vienna, 1908

—

Adolf Loos (1870–1933)

—

Following a visit to Chicago, Loos developed an admiration for the work of Wright's master, Louis Sullivan; a possible explanation for the similarity of Loos's bar to Unity Temple. The marble ceiling grid extends into mirrored imaginary space above the tiny bar. Decoration is reduced to the grain of materials and the elegant necessities of construction. Oskar Kokoschka (1886–1980) wrote, 'The tranquil discretion of this bar permitted one to lose the agitation which already pervaded the other cafés.'

Palais Stoclet, Brussels, 1905–11

—

Josef Hoffmann (1870–1956)

—

The banker Adolphe Stoclet enabled the leader of the post-Wagner generation in Vienna to create a Gesamtkunstwerk, with a freely composed exterior, influenced by Mackintosh and anticipating Art Deco, with a sumptuous interior created under the direction of the painter Gustav Klimt. The white marble sheath of the exterior hides the structure, fastened with metal angles. Mme Stoclet, daughter of a Parisian art critic and dealer, chose her husband's ties to match the floral decorations each day.

AEG Turbine Factory, Berlin, 1909

—

Peter Behrens (1868–1940)

—

Artist first, then architect and all-purpose designer, Peter Behrens was a powerful force in Germany, after becoming artistic consultant in 1907 to the large-scale production of the Allgemeine Elektricitäts-Gesellschaft, the German holder of Edison's patents since 1883. In its buildings, products and typography, Behrens aimed for Platonic purity of form. The side of the Turbine Factory shows the steel frame, while the end recalls a monumental classical portico.

Fagus Factory, Alfeld-an-der-Leine, 1911–12, extended 1914

—

Walter Gropius (1883–1969) and Adolf Meyer (1881–1929)

—

After 1891, American machinery made it economical to customize shoe sizes, and Karl Benscheidt developed shoe-last production at Alfeld as a reforming mission for German foot-health and good employment, building a model factory – initially with a local architect, until Walter Gropius's experience with Behrens won him the job. With the 1914 extension, where metal-framed glazing created transparent corners beside the office entrance, Gropius achieved his aim of 'etherialization'.

Theatre, Deutsche Werkbund Exhibition, Cologne, 1914
—
Henry van de Velde (1863–1957)
—

Starting out as a painter, van de Velde made his reputation as a designer and architect in Art Nouveau style for progressive patrons in Germany after 1900 The 1914 Deutscher Werkbund exhibition – closed early when war broke out – captured the varieties of proto-Modernism, among them van de Velde's achievement of a modern design language less rigid than that of some of his peers. Inside, the three-part stage was an innovation he was unable to repeat elsewhere. The temporary building was demolished in 1920.

Théâtre des Champs-Élysées, Avenue Montaigne, Paris, 1911–13
—
Auguste Perret (1874–1954)
—

Perret's family were specialists in reinforced concrete construction, and he was trained to work with them as architect. Intended as construction adviser to van de Velde for this project, he persuaded the client that his structural frame necessitated a redesign, pushing out his collaborator. For Perret, concrete offered a rational principle in the French tradition, bridging history and modernity. In turn, the sculptor Antoine Bourdelle (1861–1929) took over the facade design, but the theatre was still criticized as being too German.

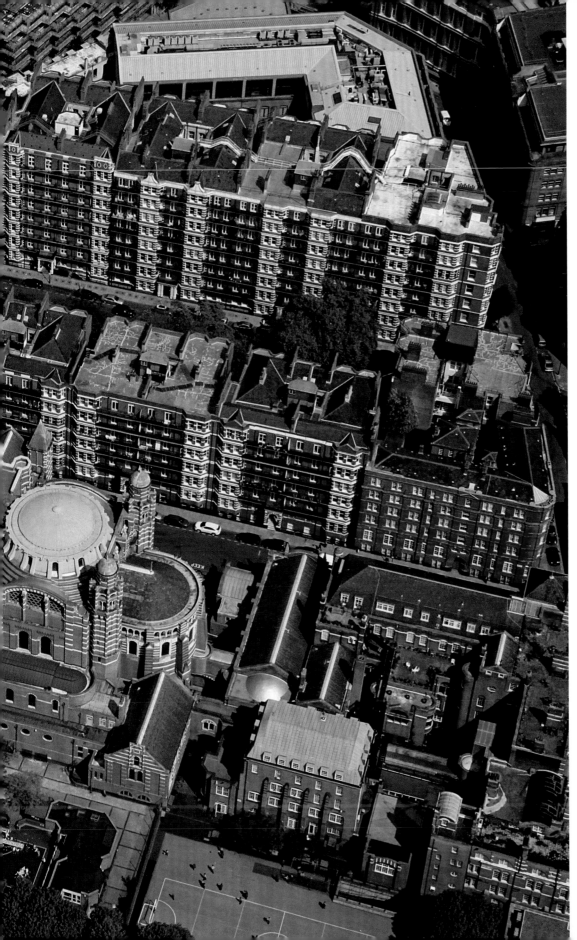

Westminster Cathedral, London, 1895–1903

—

John Francis Bentley (1839–1902)

—

Affirming the restored role of the Catholic Church in England, Bentley's cathedral, dedicated to The Most Precious Blood of Our Lord Jesus Christ, used the Byzantine style as an economical solution that allowed quick completion and later decoration. Mass concrete, without reinforcement, was used for the domed roof structure, and what was once dubbed 'Cardinal Vaughan's Railway Station' remains a numinous, lofty space, still only partially clothed in mosaic and marble, which united disparate factions in English architecture. Bentley's indeterminate 'free style' exterior was a skilful historical synthesis.

**Cathedral of St John the Divine,
Amsterdam Avenue, New York,
1892–present**
—
**George Lewis Heins (1860–1907)
and Christopher Grant LaFarge
(1862–1938), followed after 1909
by Ralph Adams Cram (1863–1942)**
—
The crossing dome by Heins and
LaFarge used patented Guastavino
tile or timbrel vaulting, a modern
reworking of a historic technique.
Intended as temporary, it remains
at the core of the massive Gothic
structure by Cram that added
nave and transepts to the early
portion shown here. Although he
sometimes used other styles, Cram
believed in the universal qualities
of Gothic design, which combined
innovative thinking about structure
with traditional stonemasonry
techniques.

26

Cathedral of St. John's Divine, New York City.

First Church of Christ Scientist, Berkeley, California, 1910–12

Bernard Maybeck (1862–1957)

'Pure Romanesque made out of Modern materials' was Bernard Maybeck's phrase for the church built in the progressive academic community at Berkeley. The design is a counterpart of Wright's Unity Temple, similar in plan, form and volume, but with exuberant colour and Gothic tracery, in which many traditions are synthesized. The concrete frontal of the reader's desk is decorated with trees to conceal faults in the casting. In the streets around are many of Maybeck's imaginative shingled timber houses.

Quarr Abbey, Isle of Wight, England, 1911–12

Dom. Paul Bellot (1876–1944)

After studying at the École des Beaux-Arts in Paris, Bellot joined the Benedictine order, becoming a member of the exiled French community of 100 at Quarr in 1901. From there, he designed and built a monastery in the Netherlands, before embarking on his only English work in a similar style of athletic, undecorated brick Gothic, with the dramatic interlaced vault over the sanctuary. In a long career, Bellot built abbeys and parish churches in Belgium, Canada, France and Portugal.

Memory, Modernity and Modernism 1890–1914

Helsinki Central Railway Station, competition 1904, construction 1910–19
—
Eliel Saarinen (1873–1950)
—
In the 1890s, Nordic countries combined elements of English Arts and Crafts and German *Jugendstil* with the massive Romanesque masonry of H. H. Richardson to replace the thin classicism that had persisted until then. In Finland, the national language and mythology were also being revived. Saarinen won the competition, but after criticism from rivals, the design became less nationalistic, with the addition of an American-style tower, but alongside four mythical globe-bearing giants.

Viceroy's House (now Rashtrapati Bhavan), New Delhi, 1912–29
—
Sir Edwin Lutyens (1869–1944)
—
In a wave of Imperial classicism before 1914, Lutyens brought stylistic open-mindedness and formal refinement to the task of representing British rule in India in a new capital city, blending Mogul and Renaissance elements above and below the *chhajja*, or deeply projecting cornice. 'Taking the best of East and West,' wrote the critic Robert Byron of Lutyens in 1931, 'bests which are complementary, he has made of them a unity and invested it with double magnificence.'

**Faculté de Médecine et de
Pharmacie, Bordeaux, 1876–88,
1902–22**
—
Jean Louis Pascal (1837–1920)
—
Pascal trained several British and
American architects in his atelier
in Paris, contributing to the spread
of admiration in the early Modernist
years for the design techniques of
the École des Beaux-Arts. He was
awarded the Gold Medal of the
Royal Institute of British Architects
in 1914, in admiration of the abiding
values of academic classicism,
seen in the long gap between the
design of the Bordeaux building
and its completion, unaffected
by passing fashion.

'La Ciudad Lineal' ('The Linear City'), 1882

—

Arturo Soria y Mata (1844–1920)

—

Soria, who was in charge of Madrid's streetcar network, published his solution to the congestion of the modern city in 1882, promoting building alongside the tracks of trains and trams, offering an alternative, more equitable and healthy form of urban development than the normal growth of suburbs, allowing for private ownership of land and houses. When a circular railway was built around Madrid to test the idea, property speculation defeated the vision, but the idea lived on.

32

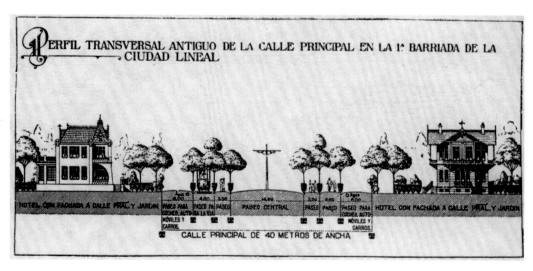

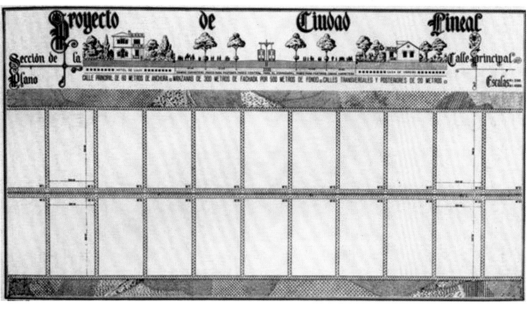

Apartments, 26 rue Vavin, Paris, 1912–13
—
Henri Sauvage (1873–1932) and Charles Sarazin (1873–1950)
—
Sauvage was engaged with cheap hygienic housing from 1904. With Sarazin, he patented the *immeuble à gradins*, with a stepped section built of concrete to give each flat a sunlit balcony and privacy, even suggesting pyramid formations. Rue Vavin (where Sauvage himself lived) and its later twin in the rue des Amiraux are both clad in white tiles. The latter used the leftover space between the sloping faces of the building to insert a swimming pool.

'Garden City', diagrammatic plan, 1898

—

Ebenezer Howard (1850–1928)

—

In *To-Morrow: A Peaceful Path to Real Reform*, 1898, the social thinker Howard described the economic and spatial basis for a new form of development combining the best aspects of town and country: zoned, serviced by rail and road, and limited to a sustainable size. The value of developed land would return to the community. Letchworth, founded in 1905, was the first example, and the subject of intense interest from planners in Germany and elsewhere.

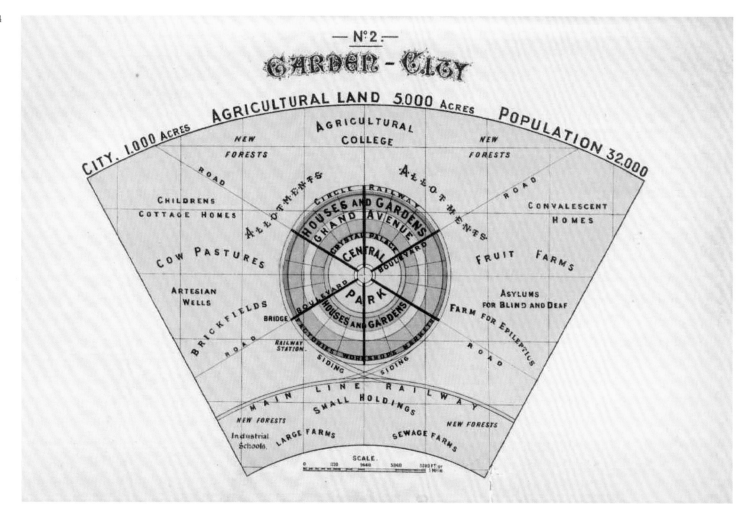

Dalcroze Institute Festspielhaus, Gartenstadt Hellerau, Dresden, 1911

—

Heinrich Tessenow (1876–1950)

—

Hellerau is the best known of the German garden cities, designed by a group of architects. Émile Jaques-Dalcroze, the Swiss exponent of eurhythmics as a physical counterpart to music training, was encouraged to settle there and teach, with Tessenow's stripped classical theatre for performances, attended by the young Le Corbusier among others. Inside, the walls could be illuminated from inside with coloured electric lights, while the stage would be set with steps and platforms designed by Adolphe Appia.

7–10 Lechfeldstrasse, Munich-Laim, 1910–11

—

Theodor Fischer (1862–1938)

—

Fischer was prominent among the German architects who were inspired by English garden cities to develop small housing settlements (*Siedlungen*) on the edge of cities. The steep roofs follow English precedent, although the arched entrances to back gardens resemble more closely German courtyard planning. Nonetheless, these projects broke the hold of the *Mietskaserne*, or rent-barracks, as the norm for working-class dwellings and set a precedent for later Modernist housing.

Proposed Civic Center, Chicago, 1909
—
Daniel H. Burnham (1846–1912), rendering by Jules Guérin (1866–1946)
—
The World's Columbian Exposition in Chicago, 1893, led to the plan of Chicago of 1909, both reflecting the Beaux-Arts influence in the USA, termed the City Beautiful movement. Grandly published with colour plates, Burnham's Chicago envisaged a city quite different to what had arisen after the 1870 fire. Led by a desire to hide road and rail below ground level, the plan also introduced radial avenues in place of the grid.

Woolworth Building,
233 Broadway, New York,
1910–13
—
Cass Gilbert (1859–1934)
—
Louis Sullivan's pioneering Midwestern skyscrapers, classical in essence, belong to the 1890s, after which the initiative passed to New York, where the Woolworth Building, celebrating a self-made retailer, overtopped the other first-generation skyscrapers. Owing to its Gothic style, a reasonable response to verticality, it was inevitably labelled a 'Cathedral of Commerce'. The steel frame was clad with cream terracotta. Owned until 1998 by the Woolworth company, it has now been converted to residential use.

2
—
Solidity
and
Scenography
—

1914—
1939

Around 1912, a generation of Nordic architects rediscovered their local neoclassical tradition – French-inspired, feminine and sophisticated in detail although severe in mass. Asplund's cinema, smaller than his painting suggests, creates a mysterious journey into the world of imagination, emerging beneath a Mediterranean night sky with Pompeian red paintwork and embroidered fronts to the balconies – colour was a major theme of the 1920s. Miraculously, it survives.

In James Joyce's *Ulysses*, published in 1922, the author's alter ego, Stephen Dedalus, declares that 'history is a nightmare from which I am trying to escape'. In an almost equally famous phrase, the American critic Van Wyck Brooks wrote in 1915 of the possibility of 'a useable past'. Architects were divided according to which view they took. A useable past suggests a critical sifting of history according to purpose, and this is how architects were able to be creative and original within the framework of recognized styles, even after Modernism might have made such overt retrospection seem irrelevant, or even dangerous.

As Modernism came into view after World War I, it appeared in many ways impractical and excessively dogmatic, and Modernists were challenged by the elegance of room sequences devised by a French master such as Paul Cret. Solidity has practical virtues – namely, insulation from temperature and noise. With the benefit of an aesthetic of primitivism and simplicity, brick and stone acquired a new expressive and emotional charge that worked at both large and small scales. New discoveries from the ancient world, such as Assyrian and Babylonian architecture, offered nuances that could replace the overworked application of Greek and Roman classicism, and contributed to the Art Deco look. These familiar revival styles were approached with greater understanding of their archaeological significance, and restraint added expressive force to the classical orders on the occasions when they were applied. Restraint was not always valued, however, and the flavour of a studio setting for a Hollywood epic was often in the air.

There was, nonetheless, a distinctive classicism during the 1920s and 1930s that was seen from the Baltic to the Mediterranean, and widely across the rest of the globe. It often took inspiration from the neoclassical simplifications of the 1790s, seeing the intervening century as a mistaken detour into eclecticism. The emotional range of this style was considerable, encompassing the overly winsome charm of 'Swedish Grace', the neurotic Mannerism of the Italian 'Novecento' style, and the less comfortable associations of Italian architecture under Fascism, and German architecture under Nazism – in both cases, continuations of existing design trends. After 1945, the *pompier* style survived in Stalinist Russia with the Moscow Metro. Auguste Perret strengthened his allegiance to the tectonic logic of classical composition, deeply rooted in the French psyche, even while using the entirely plastic material of concrete. Sculptors, muralists and other artists were welcomed as collaborators in a continuation of the Arts and Crafts spirit.

There was a less predictable efflorescence of Gothic modes – massive and primitive at times, but also prone to exuberant decoration. Thus the Chicago Tribune Tower of 1925, the result of an international competition, became a Gothic skyscraper for reasons connected with symbolic meaning in the immediate post-war period. In Germany, the construction of numerous churches nurtured a simplified version of Romanesque, in which tall planes of brickwork with round arches struck a dignified tone without bravado.

Stockholm City Hall, 1911–23

Ragnar Östberg (1866–1945)

A leading example of national romanticism, Stockholm's City Hall is built around two open spaces and, set on its corner plot, the brick facades look over one of the city's lakes. Despite its plain, largely undecorated exterior, the right-hand aspect is articulated with a row of lancet windows and, on the left an open arcade connects the courtyard and water. Decorative details include the three crowns, a historical national symbol of Sweden, mounted on the 106-metre (348-foot)-high tower.

Hilversum Town Hall, The Netherlands, 1928–31

Willem Marinus Dudok (1884–1974)

As municipal architect for the Dutch city of Hilversum, Dudok was responsible for city expansion, as well as designing houses, estates, swimming pools, parks and gardens; the city's town hall is his masterpiece. Heavily influenced by Frank Lloyd Wright's Prairie Houses, with its strong horizontal lines and monumental tower, the building consists of two squares, an inner courtyard surrounded by offices and a second courtyard surrounded by lower ranges. The mixture of voids and solid forms is unified by the skin of yellow brick, which wraps around the different components.

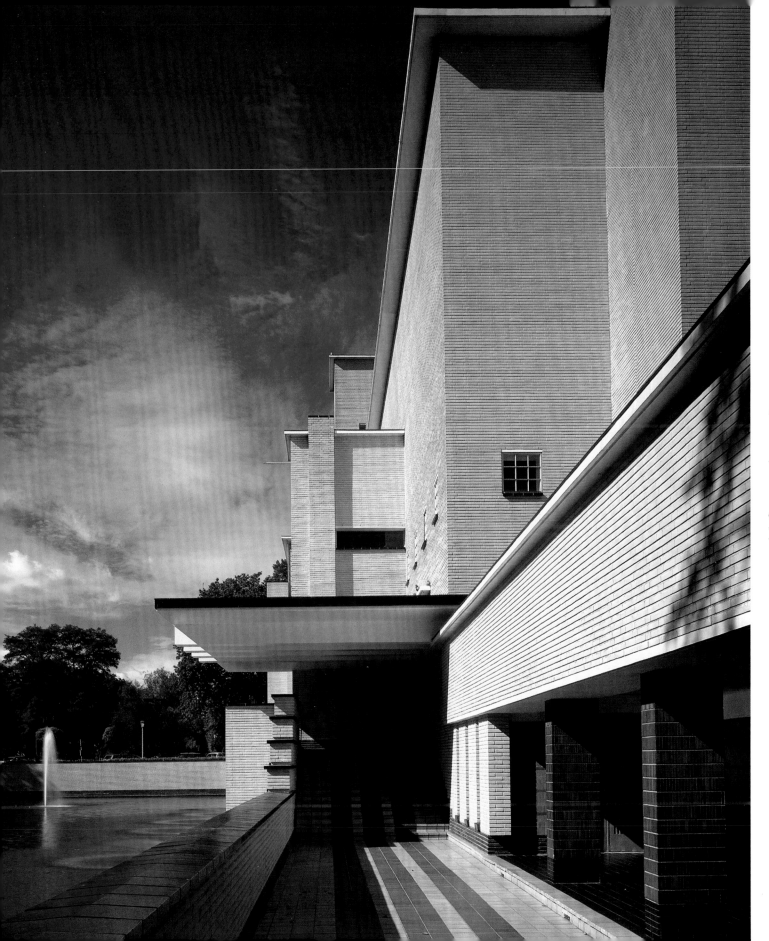

Oslo City Hall, competition 1918, execution 1931–50

—

Arnstein Arneberg (1882–1961) and Magnus Poulsson (1881–1958)

—

Symmetrical and monumental in composition, the plain brick profiles of Oslo City Hall mark the end of the era of heavyweight Nordic town halls. The architects of the Stockholm and Copenhagen town halls were among the competition judges, but the building took so long to complete that it became dated before it was finished. Carved granite figures mark the entrance, and the ceremonial interior spaces have inlaid stone floors and

patriotic murals. The Norwegian historian Christian Norberg-Schulz described the City Hall as 'a heterogeneous juxtaposition of features that reflect its long process of becoming: national romanticism, late classicism and functionalism, coupled with anachronistic artistic decoration.'

42

Nebraska State Capitol, Lincoln, competition 1920, execution 1922–32
—
Bertram Grosvenor Goodhue (1869–1924)
—
The tower, rising from the prairie and drawing on Goodhue's experience in Gothic architecture, was an innovation for a capitol that won him the Nebraska commission in the conservative US architectural climate. Goodhue described it as 'a sort of Classic, very loose no doubt … I find myself too conservative wholly to abandon the language of ornament to which I am accustomed.' The interiors are richly adorned with painting and sculpture.

National Musée des Travaux Publics (now Palais d'Iéna), Paris, 1936–48
—
Auguste Perret (1874–1954)
—
Perret boasted that there was no trace of plaster in his most classical essay in concrete construction. Intended to house displays of large machinery as part of the 1937 Exposition Internationale des Arts et Techniques dans la Vie Moderne, it provided an auditorium and three levels of galleries with slender columns of a new concrete order and a grid of ceiling beams, rational and French. The curving concrete stair circles unsupported from half-landing to first floor and bounces slightly to the tread.

Stockholm Public Library, 1921–28
—
Erik Gunnar Asplund (1885–1940)
—
Toylike and yet slightly forbidding, Asplund's library is ambiguous, showing how classicism could embed many layers of meaning and reference and still be a live medium of expressive space, with a narrow stair leading to the wide, light-filled central rotunda. Set at the edge of a rocky outcrop, the library joins city grid to wild nature while standing on the cusp between old and new architecture.

**Jules E. Mastbaum Foundation,
Rodin Museum, Benjamin Franklin
Parkway, Philadelphia, 1926–29**
—
**Paul Philippe Cret (1876–1945)
and Jacques Gréber (1882–1962)**
—
The US infatuation with French
architecture grew from the 1880s
to become the basis of teaching and
public buildings by 1900. Paul Cret
came to teach at the University of
Pennsylvania in 1903. This drawing
shows how the cross section was
crucial to French understanding
of a building's character, showing
its sequence of spaces, light and
decoration. Cret's pupils included
Louis Kahn, who carried this
aesthetic practice into Modernism.

**Faaborg Museum, Denmark,
1912–15**
—
Carl Petersen (1874–1923)
—
As a young man, Petersen set his
own agenda of studying Danish
architects and artists of a century
earlier and planning a return to
'classicism's complete mastery of
form and line', combined with the
brilliant colours of ancient Greece,
as a valid modern way of working
rather than mere eclectic copying.
The Faaborg Museum, which
included furniture in a similar
vein by Kaare Klint, was his major
work and originated the classical
revival in all the Nordic countries
after 1920.

Church of the Most Sacred Heart of Our Lord, Vinohrady, Prague, 1928–32

Jože Plečnik (1872–1957)

—

The Slovenian Plečnik was welcomed in Prague and spent his middle years there, mainly working on the city's castle. As a favourite pupil of Otto Wagner, Plečnik absorbed Semper's theories, demonstrating through a long career how classicism could be emotionally powerful without coarseness or pedantry. Semper's ideas of cladding and sheathing buildings are evident in the Sacred Heart's 'ermine cloak' of projecting reflective bricks and its stylized garlands. Plečnik's career continued in Ljubljana, where he transformed the city.

Antoniuskirche, Basel, 1925–27

Karl Moser (1860–1936)

—

As it had done for Perret, with his Notre Dame du Raincy in Paris, 1923, concrete construction offered a 65-year-old Swiss architect and academic the potential to refresh the basilican plan with an emphasis on large areas of coloured-glass windows and other fittings in a primitive 'medieval modern' spirit, continuing the collaborative ethos of *Jugendstil*. In 1928 Moser became the first president of the international Modernist meeting, CIAM.

St Kamillus, Mönchengladbach, Germany, 1929–34

Dominikus Böhm (1880–1955)

—

Böhm was a leader in simplifying church design to a reduced Romanesque, usually including great planes of brick wall and deep openings. His plans favoured communal participation in the mass, and in some cases he anticipated the reforms of the Second Vatican Council by designing churches in the round with a central altar. St Kamillus is a monastic church with a dramatic full-height screen wall dividing nave and choir, and an apse with tall, narrow windows.

St Fronleichnam, Aachen, Germany, 1929–30
—
Rudolf Schwarz (1897–1961)
—
Admired by Mies van der Rohe, Schwarz was nonetheless a severe critic of the Bauhaus. He shared Böhm's community-based liturgical thinking, and abstracted his church buildings to the simplest elements to intensify the qualities of structure, light and space, seen in the great white box at Aachen. After decades of relative neglect, Schwarz's achievement as designer and theorist is now seen as an important alternative strand in architectural history.

**Crematorium Chapel, Brno,
1925–30**
—
Arnošt Wiesner (1890–1971)
—
Brno, the principal city of Moravia,
included leading examples of
Modern architecture in the interwar
years. Wiesner was a transitional
figure who, in his most famous work,
found a point of balance between
monumental memory (ziggurats,
Gothic pinnacles) and modernity,
especially in the plain white interior,
flooded with light from concealed
sources. Wiesner moved to England
in 1939. He returned to Brno briefly
after the war, but in 1948 returned
permanently to England, where he
became an architectural teacher
at the University of Liverpool.

Novoslobodskaya Metro Station, Moscow, 1952

—

Alexey Dushkin (1904–77)

—

The Moscow Metro construction began in the early 1930s, with technical help from London. Dushkin's entry for the Palace of Soviets competition probably won this Ukrainian architect favour in Moscow, where he also designed one of the 'Seven Sisters' skyscrapers. Novoslobodskaya is 40 metres (130 feet) below ground, and Dushkin wanted to experiment with backlit stained glass, made in Latvia to designs by Pavel Korin. By 1952, this work seemed anachronistic in the West.

Stuttgart Hauptbahnhof, competition 1910, construction 1914–28

—

Paul Bonatz (1877–1956) and Friedrich Eugen Scholer (1874–1949)

—

While acknowledging the non-historical nature of station buildings, Bonatz echoed many traditional forms in an innovative asymmetrical layout, with initial classical details stripped away, in favour of overall rough stone construction. One critic declared it 'the first train station quarter in Germany, and probably the world, that is not horrible', but another linked it to Stockholm City Hall as 'among the most dangerous [buildings] that have recently been constructed'.

Arnos Grove Station, London, 1932

—

Charles Holden (1875–1960)

—

After designing underground stations in South London in the 1920s, Holden travelled with his patron, Frank Pick, to inspect European architecture with a view to a new building campaign on the Piccadilly line. In low-rise suburbs, the stations acted as civic monuments, projecting moderate progressive ideals of efficient service. Holden's experience as a free-thinking classical architect before 1914 ensured that they were finely crafted, elegant and memorable.

INA Building, EUR, Rome, 1938–52
—
Giovanni Muzio (1893–1982), with Mario Paniconi (1904–73) and Giulio Pediconi (1906–99)
—
EUR, a cultural and business quarter of Rome, was intended for the Esposizione Universale Roma of 1942, commemorating the twentieth anniversary of the Fascist regime, but the show was cancelled due to the war. Muzio made his reputation in 1920s Milan with characterful buildings with Mannerist compositions, but post-war became an equally individualistic Modernist. His contribution to EUR is indicative of a broader body of work that eliminates detail while retaining a classical essence.

**Daily News Building, 220 East
42nd Street, New York, 1929–30**

—

**John Mead Howells (1868–1959)
and Raymond Hood (1881–1934)**

—

Howells and Hood won the
Chicago Tribune Tower competition
with a Gothic design in 1922,
but Eliel Saarinen and Adolf
Loos's submissions influenced
Howells' later style of monumental
abstraction. The client's idea for
the building was simple ('all I want
is a printing press with a bit of office
space attached') yet the imposing
flat-faced tower, with setbacks
designed to conform to zoning laws,
also achieved a maximum rental
value for the site, while the incised
sculpture by Rene Chambellan
added to its promotional value.

Grattacielo Martini (Torre Piacentini), Piazza Dante, Genoa, 1935–40
—
Marcello Piacentini (1881–1960) and Angelo Invernizzi (1884–1958)
—
Piacentini's career began before 1914 as an academic classicist, but in the late 1920s he was influenced by the monumental form of American skyscrapers. He adopted a simpler, rationalist style and built city-centre office towers in Bergamo and Brescia. Favoured by Mussolini as a more conservative Modernist, Piacentini played a major role in planning the University of Rome and EUR. His Genoa tower (right in photo) adds stylish stripes to the typical pyramidal composition.

54

ROCKEFELLER CENTER
NEW YORK
NEW YORK CENTRAL LINES

Unified civic architecture was a historically based ideal of the mid-twentieth century, symbolizing the efficiency of modern culture, and John D. Rockefeller's development, started in the worst years of the Depression, was ambitious for a private scheme. It had public spaces between the buildings, coordinated with the subway and adorned with works of art, including Paul Manship's golden *Prometheus* and lobby murals by Frank Brangwyn and José María Sert.

Reconstruction of Le Havre, Normandy, France, 1945–64

—

Auguste Perret (1874–1954)

—

The Atlantic port was flattened by Allied bombing. Perret had already formed a group of younger pupils for reconstruction work, and after his death they perpetuated his rational grid style, so reminiscent of French classicism and intentionally banal. The elderly architect saved the town hall and the Church of St Joseph (1951–56) for himself, giving the latter a massive octagonal lantern tower, reflecting the synthesis of Gothic and classical in Perret's thinking.

'The Ship', Eigen Haard Housing, Spaarndammerbuurt, Amsterdam, 1917–20

—

Michel de Klerk (1884–1923) and Piet Kramer (1881–1961)

—

There was severe overcrowding in Amsterdam by the early 1900s, hence ambitious projects for new housing that de Klerk wished to individualize and humanize. The Amsterdam School of Architecture, of which he was a leader, emerged from the Dutch Gothic school of Cuypers, with echoes of Dutch colonies in Indonesia, seen in the brick spire of the triangular 'Ship' portion of the estate built by the cooperative Eigen Haard ('Own Hearth').

Cranbrook Academy of Art, Bloomfield Hills, Michigan, 1926–42
—
Eliel Saarinen (1873–1950)
—
Saarinen came second in the Chicago Tribune Tower competition in 1922, and shortly afterwards was commissioned by the Detroit newspaper publisher George G. Booth to plan an arts and crafts academy, both the building and the curriculum. Romantic in spirit but classical in form, the campus elides with the natural surroundings and has sculpture by the Swedish Carl Milles, another of the teachers. Saarinen moved with his family from Finland to oversee the project, bringing his young son, Eero, who was to become an important architect in post-war America.

3
—
The New Reality
—
1914—
1932

In a remarkable prevision of later buildings, his own among them, Mies entered a competition to design a skyscraper that would sit next to Berlin's main central railway station with this design, to be completely sheathed in glass – a technical feat never attempted before this date. The footprint is triangular, with deep insets to give daylight to the core. Avant-garde Modernism was inspired as much by such visionary proposals as by what was actually built.

From the wreckage of World War I arose the new spirit (*L'Esprit Nouveau*) of architecture with the 'new building' (*Neues Bauen*), guided by the new objectivity (*Neue Sachlichkeit*). This has been called 'The Heroic Period of Modern Architecture', and it had the hallmarks of idealism, self-sacrifice, material hardship and lack of external understanding and appreciation. Seldom has such a relatively coherent set of principles and forms spread so rapidly over an international network, connected through small magazines, exhibitions and personal encounters.

Smooth, mostly white-painted, with pure geometrical shapes and crisp angles, offsetting large areas of window against plain wall, these buildings tended to look deceptively alike. By 1932, a collection of such buildings was identifiable and given the collective name, the International Style. But style, paradoxically, was exactly what they were trying to avoid, for their approaches were as different as their destinies in the time of fragmentation and danger that followed.

What distinguished this body of work from the fitful earlier attempts to create a new style? Arguably, the aesthetic preoccupations of the visual arts of Modernism ran in parallel to provide new anti-classical compositional codes. Possibly, there was a transfer from the cutting edge of physics, with a new understanding of time and space relationships in Futurism and Cubism. Politics were in play in the new Soviet Union, where for a decade the vision of a new social order was accompanied by a radically new architectural concept, considering not only the look of a building but its contribution to different social relationships.

As succeeding decades demonstrated, some of the participants in this early upsurge of collective effort were exceptionally creative individuals with surprisingly divergent aims. Le Corbusier went on to become the paradigm of the architect as artist, always pulling a new trick that turned out, on inspection, to contain layers of precedent and meaning. Mies van der Rohe, meanwhile, went down a consistent path, guided primarily by aesthetics, in which the classical tradition as understood in Germany revealed itself as the underlying motif.

The words 'functional' and 'rational' can be loosely interchangeable, but each denotes a separate strand of design. Functional buildings were fitted like a carapace of armour to the demands of a specific 'programme', while rationalist ones offered a non-specific series of spaces based on regular repeated forms.

Some of the most memorable buildings reflected the creation of new typologies to suit new social ideas – apartment blocks in Soviet Russia with communal kitchens, laundries, crèches and workers' clubs, or the rooftop car-testing track at the Fiat plant at Lingotto in Italy. The English garden city was reimagined minus historical trimmings by Ernst May at Frankfurt, while the duty of being healthy allied the new architecture from California to the new state of Czechoslovakia and beyond. As the people of this new world might have hoped never to grow old, so the buildings were seldom constructed with an eye to the future. Some perished early, while a few survivors are nurtured like vintage cars to stave off decay and recover the inspirational qualities of their first youth.

Rusakov Workers' Club, 6 Stromynka Street, Moscow, 1927–28

—

Konstantin Melnikov (1890–1974)

—

To combat alcoholism among Soviet workers, there was a long tradition of clubs offering wholesome food and drink combined with libraries and newspapers, cinemas and lectures. Such was the Rusakov Club, with its higher auditorium seating boldly projecting over the street front, with blank walls to be used for display lettering. Melnikov taught with Ilya Golosov (see page 65) at the VKhUTEMAS School in Moscow, but did not associate with the more dogmatic Constructivist group.

**Narkomfin Communal House,
25 Novinski Boulevard, Moscow,
1928–32**
—
**Mosei Ginsburg (1892–1946)
and Ignati Milinis (1899–1974)**
—
Designed to house workers at
the People's Commission for
Finance (shortened to Narkomfin),
Ginsburg's project aimed to build
a 'social condenser', encouraging
both single-family apartments
without sub-letting, and communal
facilities for food, exercise, laundry
and childcare. The key is the much-
imitated cross section of split-level
flats on long corridors at every third
level. The building is now decayed
and threatened by redevelopment.

64

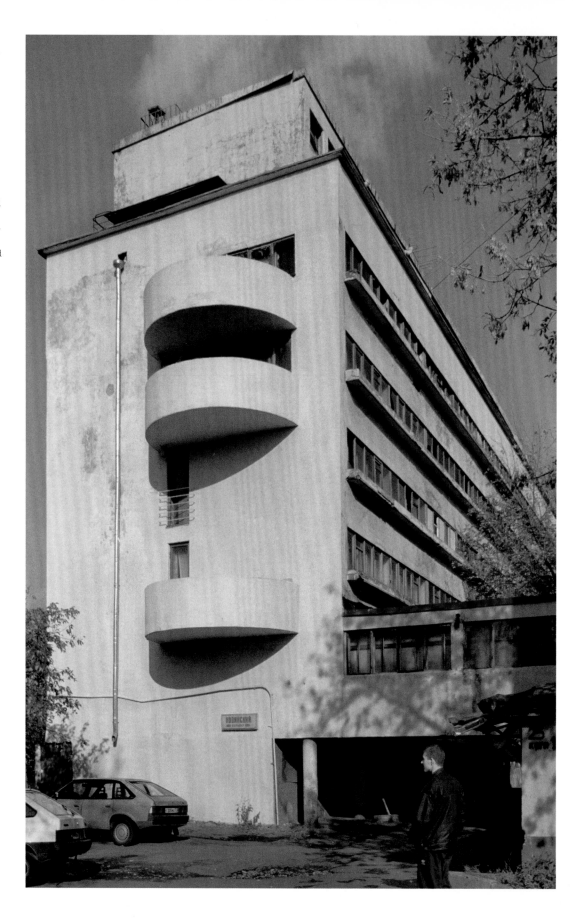

Sanatorium, Mazesta, Sochi, 1926–35
—
A. Stschussew (1873–1949)

The mud springs at Mazesta on the Black Sea were known to the Romans and favoured by Stalin. The design uses a popular modernist compositional technique of interpenetrating volumes, especially in the stair tower rising in the midst of the sun balconies. The drawing was published anonymously in the second edition of Gustav Adolf Platz's extensive collection of exemplars, *Die Baukunst der Neuesten Zeit*, 1930.

Mostorg department store, 2/48 Krasnaya Presnya Square, Moscow, 1927–28
—
Alexander Vesnin (1883–1959), Viktor Vesnin (1882–1950) and Leonid Vesnin (1880–1933)

The Vesnin brothers began their careers in Imperial Russia, catching the post-revolutionary fervour for a new way of thinking about buildings. Their Mostorg store shows the speed with which new architecture adapted existing typologies to new materials – in this case a concrete structure with large areas of glass, shown filling the whole facade in the early designs, with an undulating series of bays above the entrance. The building is now owned by Benetton.

Zuev Workers' Club, 18 Lesnaya Street, Moscow, 1927–29
—
Ilya Golosov (1883–1945)

Golosov created a striking corner composition of intersecting volumes that was widely published and was borrowed for an apartment building in Como by Giuseppe Terragni soon afterwards. The glass drum contains the staircase, giving access to the theatre that remains in use within.

Zonnestraal Sanatorium, Loosdrechtse Bos, Hilversum, The Netherlands, 1926–31
—
Johannes (Jan) Duiker (1890–1935)
—

While the Van Nelle Factory in Rotterdam (see page 68) epitomizes the universal space of a rational building, the Zonnestraal in nearby Hilversum represents functionalism, in which all the parts are tailored to a particular need. The purpose was to rehabilitate diamond workers suffering from occupational respiratory disease and TB, in surroundings of sunlight and hygiene. The building provides maximum transparency, although each room has a private sunbathing balcony. Out of use and derelict after the war, the building was restored by Wessel de Jong with exemplary care and generous government support.

66

Van Nelle Factory, Rotterdam, 1925–31

—

Johannes Brinkman (1902–49) and Leendert van der Vlugt (1894–1936)

—

The well-established Van Nelle company, which packaged and sold tea, coffee and tobacco, expanded on the edge of Rotterdam with the aim of creating an ideal factory, inspired by American ideas of efficiency to improve the lives of workers. Brinkman was an engineer and van der Vlugt an architect. The concrete frame eliminated ceiling beams by using mushroom columns, and glazing ran from floor to ceiling in the standardized structure, varied by the circular rooftop restaurant and administration wing. The building was carefully restored as the 'Van Nelle Design Factory' after 1988.

Herrmann & Steinberg Hat Factory, Luckenwalde, Germany 1921–23

—

Erich Mendelsohn (1887–1953)

—

Mendelsohn's exhibition of drawings in Berlin in 1919 launched his career, first with the famous Einstein Tower at Potsdam, followed by the factory for two hat manufacturers who decided to merge. Mendelsohn designed three tall workshops with concrete trusses and brick walls. Natural ventilation from the tall roofs drew off toxic fumes. The hat business ended in 1933, and the later factory use ended with reunification, leaving the buildings empty and at risk. Although now physically repaired, they lack a beneficial use.

Bauhaus, Dessau, 1925–26

—

Walter Gropius (1883–1969) and Adolf Meyer (1881–1929)

—

The famous design school started in Weimar in 1919 but moved to a more supportive city, offering Gropius, its founder, the opportunity to purpose-build its premises and fix its image in perpetuity. A pinwheel plan bridges a public road, with the fully glazed workshop block prominent, and the student accommodation tower just visible to the right. The scale is friendly and the interiors are enlivened by colour. Nearby, the masters' houses have been restored and, while acting as a heritage mecca, the Bauhaus also functions again as intended.

Kiefhoek Housing Estate, Rotterdam, 1925–30
—
Jacobus Johannes Pieter Oud (1890–1963)
—

A 1.5-hectare (4-acre) plot surrounded by existing housing was developed by Oud with minimal but individual terraced houses, each with a garden, an innovation for flat-dwelling Holland. The free-standing terraces meant there were no closed back courtyards, considered a health risk. Internally, curved stairs helped to save space, in accord with the campaign among the Modernist members of CIAM to achieve the most with the least amount of space. The exteriors were white but relieved with touches of bright primary colour.

Hufeisensiedlung, Britz, Berlin 1925–33
—
Bruno Taut (1880–1938), with city architect Martin Wagner (1885–1957) and garden designer Leberecht Migge (1881–1935)
—

To alleviate housing congestion in Berlin, Wagner helped to establish GEHAG, a housing association that borrowed money to build many model estates to the designs of Taut and others, on English garden city principles, with gardens for cultivation and recreation, and a mixture of flats and houses. The Hufeisensiedlung ('Horseshoe Estate') forms the centre of the Britz development, enclosing a public park. Taut used primary colours for doors and windows, now reinstated in these UNESCO-protected sites. One of the houses, authentically furnished, is available for holiday lets.

Apartment House, Weissenhofsiedlung, Stuttgart, 1927
—
Ludwig Mies van der Rohe (1886–1969)
—

In 1925, Mies's reputation ran ahead of his actual built work. The Deutscher Werkbund chose him to masterplan their exhibition housing for 1927, early Modernism's best-known collective effort at public education. His long, almost uninflected block is a backdrop to the site. Although covered with smooth white render, the steel frame allowed internal spaces to open up and offer flexibility. 'Here the fundamental anonymous character of our time is apparent,' Mies declared.

Siedlung Römerstadt, Frankfurt, 1927–28
—
Ernst May (1886–1970)
—

Ernst May performed a function similar to Taut's in Berlin (see opposite), although Frankfurt's efforts extended to recommended furnishings, garden plans and the famous standardized efficient kitchens by Margarete Schütte-Lihotzky. Römerstadt (or 'Roman Town') is the most romantic of May and his colleagues' 16 housing developments, looking down over the Nidda valley from rampart-like terraces, behind which run long rows of two-storey houses with ample trees and copious allotment gardens.

Villa Savoye, 82 rue des Villiers, Poissy, France (1929–31)

—

Le Corbusier (1887–1965) and Pierre Jeanneret (1896–1967)

—

Nicknamed 'Les Heures Claires', the villa was described by Le Corbusier as an idyllic pastoral retreat, with its living floor raised to survey distant views from a hilltop, with a pleasing ambiguity of inside and outside spaces. Like a classical villa in its compactness, it exemplifies the 'Five Points of the New Architecture' that Le Corbusier hastily set down for Stuttgart in 1927 and then mostly abandoned. Rescued from dereliction in 1964, the villa now receives streams of visiting students and tourists.

Villa Stein-De Monzie, 17 rue du Professeur Victor Pauchet, Vaucresson/Garches, France, 1926–28

—

Le Corbusier (1887–1965) and Pierre Jeanneret (1896–1967)

—

Shared between the former wife of the French construction minister and her art-loving American friends, Michael and Sarah Stein, this suburban villa gave Le Corbusier his first chance as a Modernist to build on a generous scale. The underlying structural grid of columns and floor plates supports intricate interiors, reinventing the idea of the dwelling and developing an unfolding cinematic experience of space. The terrace cut from the cubic volumes is a feature much imitated up to the present.

Villa E-1027, Rocquebrune-Cap-Martin, Alpes-Maritimes, France, 1926–29
—
Eileen Gray (1878–1976), with Jean Badovici (1893–1956)
—
Gray, an Anglo-Irish furniture designer in the Parisian avant-garde, worked with her lover Badovici, architect and magazine editor, on the design of an L-shaped seaside villa, with one large living room. They wrote, 'The interior plan should not be the accidental outcome of the façade, it must exist with a complete, harmonious and logical life of its own.' Several of Gray's furniture designs were made specially for the house, and following the rediscovery of her achievement in her final decade, have been reproduced as 'classics'.

Maison de Verre, 31 rue St-Guillaume, Paris, 1928–31
—
Pierre Chareau (1883–1950) and Bernard Bijvoet (1889–1979)
—
Hidden in a Left Bank courtyard, the gynaecologist Jean Dalsace and his wife commissioned a house in which everything was rethought for a new way of living. The ground floor is given to medical use, with the broad stair (hinged at the top and able to be raised when required) ascending to the salon around which the rooms are banked. Externally clothed in glass block, the interior is open yet full of mystery and invented gadgets. Its significance was not fully appreciated at the time, but it became a cult building when rediscovered in the 1960s.

Villa Tugendhat, Brno, 1928–30

—

**Ludwig Mies van der Rohe
(1886–1969), with Lilly Reich
(1885–1947)**

—

Cultivated industrialists commissioned Mies's mid-period masterpiece on a hilltop overlooking the Moravian capital. The house is entered from the upper level, and the visitor is taken on a journey, culminating in the panoramic view across the city, seen through a screen of windows, which can be mechanically lowered into the floor. Chrome clads and dematerializes the support columns of the great open-plan room, with its

semicircular veneered screen for the dining table, and other carefully furnished and demarcated zones. Mies's personal and professional partner, Lilly Reich, played an important role in designing the furniture and textile elements of the interior.

Doldertal Apartments, Zurich, 1935–36

—

Alfred Roth (1903–98), Emil Roth (1893–1980) and Marcel Breuer (1902–81)

—

Two cousins came together to practise in Zurich, with varied backgrounds in Modernism, and were commissioned by the historian and critic Sigfried Giedion to build in the lower part of his villa garden. Giedion consulted Breuer, one of the star pupils of the Bauhaus, then adrift after the rise of Nazism, and he proposed alterations to the original scheme that gained planning approval. The three identical blocks have an informality of composition indicative of the romantic turn in Modernism around 1935.

Schminke House, Löbau, Saxony, 1932–33

—

Hans Scharoun (1893–1972)

—

Sited close to the client's noodle factory, the Schminke House presents Scharoun's alternative approach, seeking to pick up stimuli from the site and the brief in order to add complexity and irregularity to the composition. Prominent in the short-lived Expressionist phase in Germany, Scharoun brings two alignments together, so that the external stairs and balconies play against the regular box shape. Below, the dining room enjoys a shaded panorama of outdoors, and a balcony is added for the bedroom above.

Fiat Lingotto Works, Turin, 1915–26
—
Giacomo Matté Trucco (1869–1934)
—

'In Italy, reinforced concrete came to birth early. It has found its most appropriate use so far in industrial buildings,' wrote Gustav Platz in 1930, giving the Lingotto Factory as his 'elegantly constructed' example. Designed by an engineer whose working life was devoted to the Fiat car company, the testing track on the roof created, from the need to house it on a dense site, is an enduring image of the Futurist vision of modernity expressed as speed.

**Firenze Santa Maria Novella
Station, Florence, 1932–35**

—

**Giovanni Michelucci (1891–1990)
and the Gruppo Toscano (founded
1931)**

—

Critics of an official conservative
design for this sensitive site asked
for 'the least visible form possible'.
Michelucci and a team of his
students won the design competition
with low, horizontal stone walls
and streamlined cascading glass.
The station, still in full use and
retaining its practical detailing,
represented a middle way between
traditional and avant-garde,
offering a model for insertions
in historic townscapes.

80

Casa del Fascio, Como, 1932–36

—

Giuseppe Terragni (1904–43)

—

The regular geometry of Terragni's Fascist Party municipal headquarters demonstrated the principles of rationalism, Italy's distinctive contribution to the Modern movement. Mussolini had described Fascism as 'a house of glass' where nothing was hidden. Adding a projecting concrete grid as sun shading, where party supporters could stand and face the crowds in the square, Terragni followed the idea through the atrium interior of the building and its offices behind glass walls. Later, Mussolini turned against such architectural purity, preferring monumentality.

Concert Hall, Helsingborg, Sweden, 1926–32

—

Sven Markelius (1889–1972)

Like his friend Aalto's library at Vyborg (see page 84), Markelius's concert hall began as two successive classical competition projects for a waterside site. A signatory to the Modernist manifesto *Acceptera* in 1931, Markelius was able to change the style, even after construction began. A low entrance wing, with pannier-like cloakrooms to either side, leads up to the timber-lined hall, with a restaurant below.

84

**Vyborg Library, formerly
Finland, now Russia, 1927–35**

—

Alvar Aalto (1898–1976)

—

Aalto's competition design of
1927 was classical, but by 1933,
when the commission materialized,
he had translated his spaces into
a new and more flexible design
language. The main body of the
building contains the reading rooms
and book shelving, lit by round
openings in the concrete roof slab,
with a stair emerging from ground
level into the tiered space. A lecture
room alongside it has a famous
undulating laminated timber
ceiling, similar to the shapes
of Aalto's plywood furniture.

**Lovell Health House, 4616
Dundee Drive, Los Angeles,
1927–29**

—

Richard Neutra (1892–1970)

—

After studies with Adolf Loos and
work with Mendelsohn, Neutra
moved to the USA in 1923, joining
his fellow Viennese Rudolf Schindler
in Los Angeles who had already
built for Dr Lovell, a naturopath and
media star. Here, in an appropriate
climate, the association between
Modernism and health was
rekindled. The brief replaced
bedrooms with sleeping balconies
and the swimming pool was the
social centre. The steel frame
allowed the structure to fly
overhead. A startling 15,000
people came to view the house
at its completion.

4
—
The Lost Lands of Modernism
—
1929–
1950

Czech Pavilion, Exposition Internationale des Arts et Techniques dans la Vie Moderne, Paris, 1937

—

Jaromír Krejcar (1895–1950)

—

Lightly fabricated from steel, glass and glass bricks, the Czech Pavilion, overhanging the Seine, impressed visitors with its up-to-date feel, along with the Japanese and Finnish offerings, indicating how the initiative was passing to the edges of what then seemed the core of Western culture. Its dry construction technique was a precursor to the High Tech movement.

After World War I, the map of Europe was redrawn, with the creation of new independent states, including Ireland, Czechoslovakia, Romania, Hungary, Poland and Yugoslavia, and the three Baltic states that became independent of Russia. Since the 1890s, architecture had been a means of asserting national identity through romantic regional styles. Modernism after 1920 offered the opportunity of catching up with – or even overtaking – the rest of Europe, especially in Czechoslovakia, where Prague and Brno became significant centres of Modernism, and lively magazines and manifestos challenged those of Paris.

Progressive political regimes tended to encourage Modernism, as in Spain during the brief Republican period when the GATCPAC collective flourished in Barcelona, but the civil war brought a rapid end to this phase. In Turkey, the regime of Atatürk deliberately sought to efface cultural memories and present itself as fully European. In the Communist Bloc countries after 1945, the influence of Stalin broke the continuity of the 1930s, just as it had in the USSR post-1932, leaving concrete villas, factories and sanatoria as decaying relics of a short-lived freedom. Many opportunities for Modernism existed in the form of colonial development, even if official taste tended towards the monumental. In Asmara, Eritrea, however, the Fiat Tagliero garage stands out.

Modernism was also adopted by a few pioneers in non-Western countries in preference to European academic styles, but often with an inflexion towards older indigenous cultural traditions in the use of space. While Japan's Modernist heritage is relatively well known, that of China's vast territories is still being discovered.

Since the fall of Communism in Eastern Europe in 1989–90, the picture of interwar Modernism has changed as contact between scholars has increased, archives have been opened and more cross-cultural traffic has been made possible. In addition, in 1988 a new conservation and research organization, Docomomo, was established in the Netherlands, encouraging the formation of national groups to make inventories of Modern buildings, especially those pre-dating 1939, and to report on their current condition, about which little was known at the time in the West. For those countries where no such drastic break in dialogue had occurred, such as Israel or Greece, the lack of knowledge or curiosity about early Modernism is harder to explain except in terms of a relatively small community of interest worldwide, and limited opportunities for publication. In a number of different ways, all these countries represented lost lands awaiting rediscovery.

Bringing these new histories together with old publications and the reports of émigrés of earlier generations soon made it clear that the general historiography of the Modern movement had been strongly skewed towards Western Europe. Even the literature in which this substantial body of architecture was originally presented and discussed tended to be in languages inaccessible to the majority of scholars. Only in recent years has this bias been partially corrected, with the support of new research and publication, making clear the evidence that the whole panorama of interwar architecture is more fascinating and complex than previously thought.

General Pension Institute, Winston Churchill Square, Prague, 1929–34

—

Josef Havlíček (1899–1961) and Karel Honzík (1900–66)

—

On an elevated site at the edge of the city, the Pensions Institute building is a highly disciplined formal exercise, with a four-armed cross of intersecting volumes, giving maximum daylight to the offices, and a lower block of shops. It is clad in pale buff tiles. Havlíček was an enthusiastic member of CIAM and he developed an interest in pure geometry and modular systems.

Budaörs Airport, Budapest, 1937

—

Virgil Borbiró (1893–1956) and László Králik (1879–date unknown)

—

Borbiró studied engineering and began his career as a classicist, before becoming the Hungarian delegate to CIAM. The airport was conceived in 1931, but delayed owing to the Depression. The circular terminal form was adopted during the same years, apparently independently, for the first Gatwick terminal by Hoar, Marlow and Lovett. Budaörs Airport became too small for international travel but remains in use for leisure flying.

Beach Pavilion, Rannahotell, Pärnu, Estonia, 1938–39

—

Olev Siinmaa (1881–1948)

—

Siinmaa was the city architect of Pärnu, where he designed a hotel, completed in 1937, in what was called 'Pärnu Functional Style'. The Beach Pavilion, not far from the hotel, is a simple structure made exceptional by its circular concrete platform swelling from a single support at one end, similar to a famous petrol station by Arne Jacobsen at Klampenborg, a seaside resort near Copenhagen. Pärnu is still a popular summer destination and the Beach Pavilion was restored in the 1990s.

Casa Bloc Housing, Sant Andreu, Barcelona, 1932–36

—

Josep Lluís Sert (1902–83), Josep Torres Clavé (1906–39) and Joan Baptista Subirana (1904–78) – all members of GATCPAC

—

GATCPAC (*Grup d'Arquitectes i Tècnics Catalans per a la Realització de l'Arquitectura Contemporània*), a Catalan collective of Modernists with a Spanish counterpart (GATEPAC) were a product of the Spanish Republican period, and their best-known project, the Casa Bloc, was supported by a worker's housing organization to provide low-cost housing of high quality in a poor district with communal facilities at ground level. The flats, one of which has been restored as a showpiece, are duplex, with elegant curving stairs. The building was unfinished at the outbreak of the civil war, and GATCPAC's work was censored under Franco.

**Sanatorium Machnáč,
Trenčianske Teplice, Slovakia,
1930–32**

—

Jaromír Krejcar (1895–1950)

—

With Karel Teige, Krejcar
proclaimed Constructivism in
a 1922 manifesto, but continued
to assert the artistic nature
of architecture. His sanatorium,
won in a competition, joins a
residential slab block to a lower
wing of communal facilities,
a typology seen as the same
as a left-wing collective dwelling.
The entrance is at the junction,
with an access ramp. Each of the
patients' rooms has a small railed
balcony overlooking a park by
the other side of the main block.

90

**Zelená Žaba (Green Frog) Pool
Complex, Trenčianske Teplice,
Slovakia, 1935–36**

—

Bohuslav Fuchs (1895–1972)

—

Fuchs wrote of this project in 1936,
'The thermal baths are situated
in a natural forest with cafes, a
wine cellar, an open-air swimming
pool, terraces, a bowling room,
playgrounds, sun-lit areas, and
a children's playground with a
special swimming pool. This has
all been done in a very natural
way so that the surroundings and
the structure are in harmony.'
Although restoration is intended,
the complex remains in a derelict
state at the time of writing.

I SOL· OG VANN PÅ INGIERSTRAND

VED OSLO

Ingierstrand Baths, Svartskog, Oppegård, Norway, 1934

—

Ole Lind Schistad (1891–1979) and Eyvind Moestue (1893–1977)

—

The Ingierstrand outdoor bathing station was a private development east of Oslo and served by steam ferries. It caught the mood of the 1930s with its openness and lean architecture, including a restaurant among the pines and birches, with a dancing platform similar to that at Pärnu (see page 89), and an especially high tower for the still relatively new cult of high diving – first included as an Olympic event for men and women in 1912.

Eforie – Hotel Belona

—

Eforie started as an inland health spa, specializing in mud cures, but in the 1920s was extended to the shore of the Black Sea and laid out by George Cantacuzino, the designer of its two hotels and numerous villas. He had studied at the Ecole des Beaux-Arts and sought a thoughtful middle way between historical styles and Modernism. The Hotel Bellona was originally built for a war veterans charity, but was soon converted into a hotel. Although altered, it survives, unlike many of his other buildings at Eforie.

The Blue Building (Antonopoulos Building), Exarcheia Square, Athens, 1932–33

—

Kyriakos Panyiotakos (1902–82)

—

This large, centrally located block was favoured by artistic tenants. It was meticulously equipped with built-in furniture and, unusually, provided bay windows. A large communal room on the roof terrace bonded the inhabitants in the difficult years after its construction. The original bright ultramarine colour, combined with raw sienna, was the result of a collaboration with the painter Spyros Papaloukos. Le Corbusier visited during the 1933 CIAM conference in Athens and gave his approval.

94

Low-Cost Apartment Block, Schnirchova, Prague, 1937
—
Eugene Rosenberg (1907–90)
—

'From an aesthetic point of view, Rosenberg's houses introduce many new aspects to Prague modern architecture,' wrote the critic Emanuel Hruška. 'While fully accepting the totality of the conception, much attention is paid to the perfection of details, both technically and formally. The apartment buildings represent a great contribution to and a new stimulation for our building industry.' Rosenberg, who was Jewish, managed to escape to England in 1938, and had a successful post-war career in the firm Yorke Rosenberg Mardall.

National Mint of Portugal, 1934–38

Jorge de Almeida Segurado (1898–1990) and Antonio Varela (1903–62)
—

Although somewhat cautious in style when compared to buildings in other countries in Europe in the mid-1930s, the Mint Building marked a significant development in Portugal. It occupies a complete urban block, with a central courtyard garden. The entrance at the angle makes a ceremonial approach, but it is the workers rather than the state who are pictured in the sculptural relief on the bare brick wall. One of the subsidiary entrances is marked by three-dimensional sans serif lettering, part of the lively Modernist lettering tradition of Lisbon.

School, Degania Kibbutz, Israel, 1928–30

Richard Kauffmann (1887–1958)
—

After studying in Munich with Theodor Fischer, Kauffmann was called to Palestine in 1920, during the period of the British Mandate by the economist and sociologist Arthur Ruppin, with the particular task of building rural settlements organized as *kibbutzim*, or collective farms. Kauffmann abandoned the vernacular styles previously favoured and was influential in making Modernism the mainstream style of the nascent state. The Degania school has ventilation slots above the windows, and the deep overhanging roof provides shade. An outdoor classroom and sleeping porch are included.

Atatürk's House at Florya, Istanbul, 1935

—

Seyfi Arkan (1903–66)

—

Arkan went to Germany to study under Hans Poelzig, returning in 1933 to become personal architect to the president, Mustafa Kemal Atatürk, and a chief promoter of Modernism in Turkey. Atatürk's beach house was within view of the crowds, to whom he would wave, and go swimming or rowing among them to assert his democratic nature. The house opened as a museum in 1993.

Fiat Tagliero Service Station, Asmara, Eritrea, 1938

—

**Giuseppe Pettazzi
(dates unknown)**

—

Eritrea became an Italian colony in 1890. Over the next five decades, infrastructure improvements were made and the highland town of Asmara rebuilt as the capital. Pettazzi's service station is the most spectacular of a group of 1930s buildings by expatriate Italian architects that survived during post-war years of conflict and have been recognized as a time capsule of slightly Art Deco Modernism.

Kenwood House, Kimathi Street, Nairobi, Kenya, 1937

—

Ernst May (1886–1970)

—

May's journeys are representative of the way that Modernists sought work in more remote parts of the world – starting with Russia in 1930, where expected work failed to materialize, then, after the rise of Nazism, a farm in Tanzania, before moving to neighbouring Kenya in 1937 and finding work with British associates. Kenwood House is a product of this period, a mixed residential and office building notable for its undulating wall, echoed in the deep projecting sunshades. It also has an elegant spiral staircase made of glass bricks. In 1953, May returned to Germany to work in Hamburg.

Bank of China, Hongkou Branch, Shanghai, 1933
—
Luke Him Sau (1904–91)
—
Born in Hong Kong, Luke Him Sau joined a local English architecture and engineering firm before studying at the Architectural Association in London. At the end of his course, he was chosen by Bank of China officials visiting London and became their architect for a series of buildings in the main Chinese cities. This branch in the northern part of Shanghai had a narrow site.

Wasaka House, Tokyo, 1939
—
Sutemi Horiguchi (1895–1984)
—
Japanese architecture made an important contribution to the aesthetics of Modernism, yet in Japan, Western eclecticism was dominant between the wars. Horiguchi met Mendelsohn, Gropius, Hoffmann and Oud while travelling in Europe in 1923, and, specializing in the design of tea houses on his return, aimed to synthesize his national traditions with new European ideas, especially those of Dutch rural houses and the use of earthquake-proof concrete construction.

Women's Dormitory, Beijing, 1935
—
Liang Sicheng (1901–72) and Lin Huiyin (1904–55)
—
The architects were a married couple, Lin Huiyin being the first woman architect in China and also a well-known poet, who studied in London and the USA before returning to China and setting up, with her husband (a graduate of Penn State), the architecture department at Northeastern University. After the Japanese invasion of Manchuria in 1931, they became researchers in the history of Chinese architecture based in Beijing, and designed buildings for Northeastern University, including the Women's Dormitory, an indication of social as well as architectural progress.

**Majestic Theatre staircase,
Shanghai, 1941**
—
**Fan Wenzhao (Robert Fan,
1893–1979)**
—
Like many Chinese architects
of his generation, Fan Wenzhao
studied at the University of
Pennsylvania under Paul Cret.
In the Majestic Theatre, he
departed from his previous
adherence to classical styles
and created a smooth,
streamlined foyer notably
lacking in applied decoration.

Stanhill, 34 Queens Road, Melbourne, 1942–50
—
Frederick Romberg (1913–92)

Born of German parents in China, Romberg studied at the ETH in Zurich and joined the local office of Otto Salvisberg. He migrated to Australia in 1938 and started a practice in Melbourne, before joining two local architects, Roy Grounds and Robin Boyd, in a famous partnership in 1953. Stanhill brought to Australia the latest phase of European design, backed by Romberg's thorough training in concrete construction.

Stern House, Lower Houghton, Johannesburg, 1935
—
Martienssen, Fassler & Cooke (Rex Martienssen, 1905–42, John Fassler, 1910–71, and Bernard Stanley Cooke, 1911–2011)
—
Trained among traditionalists, far from Europe, Rex Martienssen nonetheless succeeded almost single-handedly in creating the South African architectural avant-garde, with two buildings designed in a short-lived partnership (Martienssen, Fassler & Cooke), the Peterhouse Apartments, and the House Stern, both in Johannesburg, both in 1935. Le Corbusier, on whose work the designs are clearly modelled, acknowledged Martienssen's talent, which was expressed in his short life through teaching and writing as well as design.

Kahn House, 53 Trelissick Crescent, Ngaio, Wellington, New Zealand, 1940–41
—
Ernst Plischke (1903–92)
—
Plischke brought experience of study in his native Vienna (with Oskar Strnad and Josef Frank) and in America with Ely Jacques Kahn and Frank Lloyd Wright, before establishing a reputation in Austria. In 1939, he emigrated to New Zealand with his wife Anna, a garden designer. The Kahn House, built for an émigré couple, contained two bedrooms and a large living space adaptable as a private theatre. It was built of timber on a hilltop site with an expanse of windows beneath a deep overhanging roof.

Rose Seidler House, 71 Clissold Road, Sydney, 1948–50
—
Harry Seidler (1923–2006)
—
Leaving Austria for England in 1938 at the time of the Anschluss, Seidler studied first in Winnepeg and then at Harvard under Marcel Breuer and Walter Gropius. He brought European–American influences to Australia in 1948, building this house for his parents on arrival in a style reminiscent of Breuer's clear floating cubes of the time, with their open plans and typical rough stone 'feature' fireplace walls. The house became a museum in 1988 and stimulated the recognition of Modernist heritage in Australia, where Seidler made the remainder of his career, extending into the 1980s.

5
—
Other Modern: Romanticism and Revision
—
1933–1945

Sketch designs such as this record an architect's private moments of creativity. With freedom of line, Aalto's thinking about the form in relation to landscape is captured in plan, showing the two-sided courtyard, reminiscent of traditional Finnish farmsteads, with a separate art gallery, replaced by a sauna in the actual project. The cross sections show how Frank Lloyd Wright's Fallingwater was on his mind – an influence modified in the final design. The swooping curve is like his famous Savoy glass vase.

Modernism in the two decades between the world wars often seems like a slow motion film. Somewhere around the halfway point, the mood changes and the characters from the first part behave in different ways, while new actors appear and alter the plot. It is still difficult to find a universal explanation for this change, which could be described as a Romantic turn in contrast to the more mechanistic basis of the 1920s. In the process, the constants, such as smooth white walls and flat roofs that defined the earlier phase, gave way to a greater variety of materials, reintroducing texture and sometimes recalling more traditional forms. It might have been pragmatism – realizing that weather conditions made the white cubes expensive to maintain and the flat roofs a hostage to rain; or a desire to reconnect with a sense of regional character and landscape context without losing Modernism's lessons of freedom of space and composition, and thus win the sympathy of the public. For others, it may have represented loss of faith in a purely scientific approach and a greater understanding of the organic and biological as metaphors for human mutability and engagement.

Frank Lloyd Wright, who never abandoned Romanticism, owed his philosophy to Ralph Waldo Emerson and his belief in the ultimate power of nature. By contrast, Wright saw European Modernism as the corrupted child of his own early work. After becoming relatively invisible in the 1920s, he recaptured the world stage in the 1930s with Fallingwater. After 1930, having popularized the white cube look, Le Corbusier moved towards a mixture of materials and sculptural shapes, incorporating rough timber and rubble stone, influenced by Surrealism and admiration for the simple lives of peasant farmers. A new freedom of form and materials spread through the work of many architects in the following generation.

The most concerted demonstration of this Romantic turn came in the Nordic countries and Switzerland, where the history of Modernism played out in accelerated form within the single decade of the 1930s, moving from the 'International Modern', represented by Alvar Aalto's Paimio Sanatorium, to a greater use of texture, suggesting the forests and lakes of Finland. Asplund and his contemporaries in Sweden made the same transition, and Denmark became one of the most admired countries in the architectural and design world. While Modernism had always displayed an interest in a contemplative relationship between indoors and out, this wider palette of materials was linked to less formal planning and a more direct response to natural surroundings through landscape.

The critic Henry-Russell Hitchcock, writing in 1946, disapproved of the dilution of 'the intensely concentrated and boldly argumentative structural, functional and plastic statements the masters made in their great early works', but recognized that architecture had been democratized by this transformation.

Kollegienhaus, University of Basel, 1937–39
—
Roland Rohn (1905–71)
—

'One of the most ingratiating campus blocks one could happen upon,' wrote the American photographer George Kidder Smith of this three-sided courtyard complex by an architect now scarcely remembered. After the sound and fury of Modernism in the 1920s was over, it was possible to focus more on the experience of being in a building such as this, which did not strain for effect, and to enjoy its relationship to nature, where old trees were preserved.

106

Installation drawing, Golden Gate Exhibition, 1939

Josef Frank (1885–1967)

The significance of Josef Frank as a critic of Modernism from inside the movement is increasingly recognized. He developed the Viennese focus on interior design to create intimacy and tactile pleasure with natural simplicity. Decoration and pattern were admitted, especially in carpets and printed curtains and covers, many of which Frank designed for Svenskt Tenn, the company that drew him to emigrate to Sweden in 1933, and which are still in production. At the Golden Gate and the New York World's Fair, both in 1939, the Swedish Modern style made a huge impact on the American public.

Library of the Canton Ticino, Via Cattaneo, Lugano, Switzerland, 1939–41

Rino Tami (1908–94) and Carlo Tami (1898–1993)

Described as the foundational building for Modernism in Ticino, the library reflects Rino Tami's studies in Italy with Piacentini, and then in Zurich. The plan is L-shaped, with a welcoming entrance and terrace overlooking the lake of Lugano, flanked by the storage stack wing, and its concrete grid of windows takes on a rationalist character in contrast to the rest of the design.

Town Hall Watertower, Kornwestheim, Germany, 1933–35

—

Paul Bonatz (1877–1956)

—

The Town Hall is a hybrid building, with a pitched roof administration wing (palatable to the newly arrived Nazi government) and a tower that is Modernist in its concept of a concrete frame infilled with brick. The sides lean inwards at an angle of 10 degrees, and the concrete verticals get thinner as they go up. The simple segmental brick arches over the windows that lead up to the watertank are a form that remained popular into the 1960s.

Modernism and monumentality were engaged in a cautious relationship in the late 1930s, exemplified by the city hall of Denmark's university town, initially criticized for its lack of traditional features. Jacobsen and Møller added the tower as a free-standing reminiscence of Italy, but left it skeletal and clad the walls in Norwegian granite, transported with difficulty during the war. The serene atrium inside was inspired by Asplund's work in Gothenburg (see page 110).

Gothenburg Law Courts, Sweden, 1934–37

—

Erik Gunnar Asplund (1885–1940)

Adding to the existing three-sided classical building, Asplund opened his extension to the courtyard and created a light-filled atrium, acting as waiting space for the courts on the upper level. The long stair has a shallow 'going' to calm people down, and the transparent lift cage offers alternative ascent. Timber panelling creates a natural effect, and the court rooms are relatively informal. The English architect Oliver Hill wrote, 'This building exemplifies the stimulating and vital qualities of the [Modern] style at its maturity.'

The Woodland Crematorium, Skogskyrkogården (Woodland Cemetery), Stockholm, 1935–40

—

Erik Gunnar Asplund (1885–1940), sculpture by John Lundqvist (1882–1972)

—

Between Stockholm Public Library (see page 44) and his Woodland Crematorium, Asplund travelled into Modernism and then part way back. Visitors approaching up a gentle hill see the portico against the sky and the path leads them under it, where the roof opens to the sky and the figure group by Lundqvist introduces the idea of resurrection. Thus the idea of the *impluvium* from Roman houses returns in a new context, acting as a pivot to turn you leftwards to enter the crematorium, with its stone floor sloping downhill, exquisitely furnished with specially designed lighting.

Villa Konow, 43 Kråkenes Road, Bergen, Norway, 1936
—
Frederik Konow Lund (1889–1970)
—
After studying in Dresden and the USA, Lund returned to his native Norway, where he was one of the founders of the Romantic Bergen school. He developed a whole-family property with villas to his own design, the most famous being the Villa Konow, a building that could be imagined equally as a work of the late twentieth or early twenty-first century, with its attention to local materials and building traditions, and the way it grows out of the ground, rather than the typical characteristics of the 1930s.

Villa Stenersen, 10C Tuengen Allé, Oslo, Norway, 1937–39

—

Arne Korsmo (1900–68)

—

In 1928, Korsmo broke away from his traditional training and embraced Modernism, building its key Norwegian example in this suburban villa for a financier. Corbusian models are adapted to create a lighter effect than any of the originals, with a playful range of colours (the sunblind is orange) and a mixture of clear glass and glass block within the grid of the facade. The villa was given to the nation by Mr Sternersen; it is now used by the National Museum for educational purposes and is open to the public.

Baker House, Massachusetts Institute of Technology, Cambridge, 1945–49
—
Alvar Aalto (1898–1976)
—
Aalto started teaching in short bursts at MIT in 1945, and the commission for a student dormitory came from William Wurster, the architecture dean. Overlooking the Charles River, the building aims to balance privacy and sociability, giving all rooms equally good light and views by means of the undulating plan. Most remarkable perhaps was the decision to use all the bricks produced by a near-bankrupt company, including misshapen and over-fired ones, to produce the opposite of a precise mechanical wall.

Villa Mairea, Noormarkku, Finland, 1938–39

—

Alvar Aalto (1898–1976)

—

This villa was named after the art collector and patron Maire Gullichsen (née Ahlström), who was one of the founders of the Artek company, manufacturers of Aalto's wooden furniture. Aalto also designed a factory and housing for them. The exterior looks like a loose assembly of parts but is carefully calculated, while the interior flows up and around steps and stairs, with growing plants evoking the experience of the forest.

Resurrection Chapel, Turku, Finland, 1938–41

—

Erik Bryggman (1891–1955)

—

Starting, like so many of his contemporaries, under the influence of Italian vernacular, Bryggman turned to Modernism at the end of the 1920s, working with Aalto on exhibition projects. The chapel stands in woodland with a plain exterior, but opens out into a tall, curved space with plaster applied roughly using traditional techniques. To the right, the low aisle has a completely glazed wall. Nature is brought indoors with plants growing on the east wall, where a mural was intended but never executed.

De La Warr Pavilion, Bexhill-on-Sea, East Sussex, England, 1934–35

—

Erich Mendelsohn (1887–1953) and Serge Chermayeff (1900–96)

—

Mendelsohn came to England as a refugee in 1933, joining the Russian-born Chermayeff. Their seaside entertainment building was won in competition and allowed the crowds to experience modern spaces and furnishings. The sweeping stair in its projecting bay was a gesture typical of Mendelsohn, who left soon after for Palestine and then the USA. The pavilion continues as a concert and arts venue, or just a place to sit in an Aalto chair and look out to sea.

Finsbury Health Centre, Pine Street, London, 1935–38 (poster created in 1942)
—
Berthold Lubetkin (1901–90) and Tecton (founded 1932); artist Abram Games (1914–96)
—
An émigré from Georgia, Lubetkin was the most exciting Modernist in England after arriving in 1932 and setting up the Tecton partnership. His Health Centre was innovative socially, technically and aesthetically, although axially symmetrical in plan. This deliberately formal civic building, indicated Lubetkin's desire to add layers of reference and complexity to Modernism. The image was a wartime poster, withdrawn after Winston Churchill objected to showing a child with rickets.

Haifa Municipal Hospital (now Rambam Health Care Campus), Israel, 1938
—
Erich Mendelsohn (1887–1953)
—
Mendelsohn felt committed to helping the construction of a new Jewish state, and received generous commissions. Enclosing spaces between different parts of the complex on the beautiful beach site, he took care to preserve existing trees and plant gardens, writing that he was 'trying to achieve a union between Prussianism and the life cycle of Muezzin. Between anti-nature and harmony with nature.' Passive cooling techniques were incorporated, although not wholly successful.

**Fallingwater, Bear Run,
Pittsburgh, Pennsylvania,
1933–37**

—
Frank Lloyd Wright (1867–1959)
—

Wright influenced at least two
generations of younger architects,
first with his Chicago houses
and then with Fallingwater, his
'comeback' building, responding
(although he was unwilling to admit
it) to the direction taken in Europe
while opening up new possibilities.
As the architect Paul Rudolph wrote,
'Fallingwater is a realized dream.
It touches something deep within
us about which, finally, none
of us can speak.'

**Johnson Wax Administration
Building, Racine, Wisconsin,
1936–39**
—
Frank Lloyd Wright (1867–1959)
—
Wright's new creative energy
continued in Johnson Wax, unlike
anything he had built before,
although, like his Larkin Building
in Buffalo (1904) a working
environment isolated from contact
with the external world. A forest
of concrete columns is spanned
by lines of glass tubing, the whole
wrapped in smooth and curving red
brick. The furniture was designed
to match the building in colour
and style, and Wright added a slim
laboratory tower to the side.

**Model for Arnstein House,
714 Rua Canadá, São Paulo,
1939–41**

—

Bernard Rudofsky (1905–88)

—

Viennese-born Rudofsky worked
in Italy and Brazil before settling
in the USA and making his
name with exhibitions, above all
'Architecture without Architects'
(1964), the culmination of his
interest in the vernacular. João
Arnstein was a refugee from
Trieste and welcomed the single-
storey courtyard layout with
'outdoor rooms', which a critic
declared 'about as lovely a place
to live in as could be found in
the Americas'. Courtyard plans
became popular in the 1960s.

**Carver Court, Coatesville,
Pennsylvania, 1941–43**
—
**George Howe (1886–1955),
Oscar Stonorov (1905–70)
and Louis Kahn (1901–74)**
—
A senior Philadelphia Modernist,
Howe formed a partnership with
two younger architects to build
emergency wartime housing
for African-American workers
at Coatesville. This was also an
experiment in alternative living
arrangements, with the normal
functions of the American basement
raised to ground-floor level, allowing
space to pass under the blocks
and thus eliminate the distinction
between front and back. Three-
bedroom flats above are joined to
make terraces of four units and thus
to create a sense of enclosure
around the looped road of
a former racecourse.

6
—
The New World
—
1945–
1970

A project for holiday apartments by the Mediterranean exemplified the post-war idea of widened access to the fundamental pleasures of life, assisted by Modern architecture and entwined with nature. Having implanted the idea of a machine-based architecture in the 1920s, Le Corbusier moved away from this image before the war with a nostalgia for primitive forms and rough-surfaced materials. The stacked, terraced cross section of this unbuilt scheme proved highly influential for a younger generation of architects.

World War II pushed most architecture to the remoter parts of the world, such as South America, 'for the duration', but as it ended, the need for physical and social reconstruction in Europe seemed to offer opportunities on a scale beyond what seemed achievable in the turbulent 1930s. If the 1920s were the vigorous youth of Modernism, then the 1950s and 1960s represented a coming of age and maturity. This was literally true in respect of the generation of 'masters' and 'form givers' such as Frank Lloyd Wright, Le Corbusier and Mies van der Rohe, on whose example the rest of the profession depended for guidance. It was also true in the sense that an evolutionary pattern could still be discerned that seemed to validate the narrative of Modernism as a shift from avant-garde to mainstream. The principles of the movement now prevailed over survivals of academic styles for purposes of state and commerce, as if the long 'battle' for dominance was definitively won.

The reality is, of course, more complex. Modernism was never a monolithic set of principles, and there were divisions, factions and figures doing interesting things at the margins of geography and style. If the later work of Mies van der Rohe in America gave the world a standard method and aesthetic that could be readily reproduced, Le Corbusier surprised his followers with the Romantic curved forms of the chapel at Ronchamp, and by the enthusiasm with which he worked for such an old-fashioned institution as the Catholic Church. In fact, there was a resurgence of faith and church building became one of the more fruitful areas for architectural expression as cities were reconstructed, seen in the late work of Sigurd Lewerentz.

The *tabula rasa* of a style-less style could simply create boredom. Within Italian Modernism, quirky formal languages similar to sixteenth-century Mannerism gave variety and interest, especially to buildings in historic settings, while in France Fernand Pouillon's monumental stone frames for middle-income housing demonstrated that lightweight clip-on architecture was not the only economic option.

Other building types – art galleries, concert halls and even rail stations and airline terminals – took on the air of religious buildings, offering a choreographed pathway and inducing a sense of wonder at the capacity of concrete to cover large spaces and modulate light. A new form of Expressionism returned to architecture, echoing the brief phase of anti-rationalist design in the 1920s, and reaffirming the essentially artistic nature of architecture, even when, like Stirling and Gowan's Leicester Engineering Building, the explanation for the forms was given in strictly functionalist terms.

A younger generation, some of whom created Team 10 as a breakaway from CIAM, aimed for an abrasive authenticity inspired by the *art brut* movement and often expressed in *béton brut*, the French term for uncoated concrete. The term 'Brutalist' began to circulate around 1952 to describe the new tendency that, in addition to aesthetics, represented a strong commitment to stimulating human experience in the increasingly alienating cityscapes of modernity.

Unité d'Habitation, 280 boulevard Michelet, Marseilles, 1945–52

Le Corbusier (1887–1965), with Atelier des Bâtisseurs (ATBAT) – André Wogenscky (1916–2004) and engineer Vladimir Bodiansky (1894–1966)

—

Le Corbusier was 63 when he was commissioned by the Minister of Housing to build his slab block (the first of three) with 337 duplex flats crossing over access corridors in the middle of the building, similar to the Narkomfin (see page 64) allowing for double-height rooms within the narrow box shape. A street of shops was inserted halfway up, and on the roof a nursery school and running track. The concrete frame was left rough (*béton brut*, hence Brutalism), but painted with strong primary colours. Proportions were controlled by the Modulor scale.

The High Court, Chandigargh, Punjab, 1953–58

—

Le Corbusier (1887–1965) and Pierre Jeanneret (1896–1967)

—

Nehru, the first president of independent India, commissioned designs for a new capital for the state of Punjab. Coming late to the task, Le Corbusier planned the layout to include a capitol for government buildings. As at Marseilles, he included sun-breaking box-like walls beneath a concave 'parasol' roof.

Notre Dame du Haut, Ronchamp, Haute-Saône, France, 1950–55

—

Le Corbusier (1887–1965)

—

Symbol of the turn from rationalism to symbolism in post-war architecture, Le Corbusier's replacement for a war-damaged pilgrimage chapel surprised his admirers but reflected his youthful interest in world religions and esoteric beliefs. The interior has corresponding curved walls with light tipping down the brightly coloured interiors of towers. The outdoor pulpit allows for open-air services.

St Peter's, Klippan, Skåne, Sweden, 1963–66
—
Sigurd Lewerentz (1885–1975)
—

Having been, like his contemporary
Asplund, a classicist and then
a Modernist, Lewerentz ended his
career with this church complex
in a small town. Brick is the
dominant material, treated with
deliberate roughness, with patterns
improvised on site. It was a return
to architectural sensuality in pursuit
of spiritual aims. The interior is
a dark cave of brick, with steel
beams, and became one of the most
influential designs for a generation
of architects hardly born when
it was completed.

Seagram Building, 375 Park Avenue, between 52nd and 53rd Streets, New York, 1954–58
—
Ludwig Mies van der Rohe (1886–1969), with interiors by Philip Johnson (1906–2005)
—
Samuel Bronfman, company president, was persuaded by his architecturally aware daughter Phyllis Lambert to chose Mies, giving generous backing to the fulfilment of his 1920s skyscraper projects. It was one of the most influential buildings of its time, providing a standard model for office towers and plazas, so that it has become hard to appreciate the special qualities of the original, exhibiting Mies's principles of *beinahe nichts* ('nearly nothing') and 'Less is More'.

130

Solomon R. Guggenheim Museum, Fifth Avenue, between East 88th and East 89th Streets, New York, 1943–59
—
Frank Lloyd Wright (1867–1959)
—
Hilla Rebay, a German countess who inspired the elderly Guggenheim to a love of abstract art, chose Wright to design a 'temple' in New York, an inverted ziggurat with a spiral path to denote artistic progress, but also a social space. Although the building was somewhat curtailed in execution, Wright still succeeded in creating the first museum more famous for its building than its collection, whose interior was 'similar to that made by a still wave, never breaking, never offering resistance or finality to vision'.

National Congress, Brasília, 1956–60

—

Oscar Niemeyer (1907–2012)

—

Niemeyer's patron at Pampulha, Juscelino Kubitschek, became president in 1954 and he decreed a new capital, planned by Niemeyer with Lúcio Costa, on a basis of car travel, with monumental government buildings. As at Chandigargh (see page 127), these stand in isolation as objects of admiration. The twin towers of the Secretariat form a landmark, while the saucer shapes mark the two legislative assemblies, raised as if on a platform. Like other Modernist new towns, Brasília was severely criticized as inhuman, yet it sustains a loyal population.

Church of St Francis of Assisi, Pampulha, Brazil, 1943

—

Oscar Niemeyer (1907–2012)

—

Pampulha is a suburb of Belo Horizonte, all built around a reservoir to Niemeyer's designs, including a casino, dance hall and church, all part of the upsurge of optimism in mid-century Brazil. All use curved forms, directly associated with female form but also part of the colonial Baroque legacy. The east wall of the church is decorated with traditional blue-and-white tiles, and the curving roof uses shell concrete, a new discovery in which the curves strengthen the thin membrane.

**UNESCO House, Place de
Fontenoy, Paris, 1953–58**
—
**Marcel Breuer (1902–81), Pier
Luigi Nervi (1891–1979) and
Bernard Zehrfuss (1911–96)**
—
Following the complex multi-
author UN building in New York,
the cultural arm of the UN in Paris
was a simpler project, essentially
by Breuer with Nervi's engineering
input. Breuer's liking for curves
dated back to the 1930s, making
a Y-shaped building here to fit the
street pattern. The sculpture by
Henry Moore perfectly matches
the fplan shape. Inside are more
artworks by Picasso, Miró and
others, including a garden by the
Japanese-American sculptor
Isamu Noguchi.

**Stazione Termini, Rome,
1948–50**
—
**Gruppo Montuori (Eugenio
Montuori, 1907–82) and Gruppo
Vitellozzi (Annibale Vitellozzi,
1902–90)**
—
Montuori built the railway station
in Sofia in 1940, and won equal
first prize with Vitellozzi's group
in a competition of 1947, filling the
gap left when the 1872 station was
demolished to make a new arrival
point for the cancelled 1942 EUR
exhibition (see page 52), part of
which had to be incorporated. This
was a team effort, like the Royal
Festival Hall in London, a symbol
of democracy at work as Italy was
taken again into the heart of the
Anglophone world. As writer and
photographer George Kidder Smith
wrote, 'architecture, sunshine and
movement all combine to make this
the finest station entry in Europe'.

Royal Festival Hall, South Bank, London, 1948–51

—

London County Council, Robert Matthew (1906–75), Leslie Martin (1908–2000) and Peter Moro (1911–98)

—

The Festival of Britain, held in the summer of 1951 (whose mainly temporary buildings are seen in the background of the photo) was the occasion for building a new concert hall for London, from which the pent-up ideas of 15 years of wartime austerity and its aftermath burst forth in a collaborative team effort, with the concept shaped by Matthew and Martin, both to become leading administrators and educators, and Moro, an émigré former assistant to Lubetkin, who was responsible for the original elevations and well-appointed interiors with unprecedented openness and almost Baroque spatial verve.

Torre Velasca, Milan, 1956–58
—
BBPR – Gian Luigi Banfi (1910–45), Ludovico Barbaiano di Belgiojoso (1909–2004), Enrico Peressutti (1908–76) and Ernesto Nathan Rogers (1909–69)
—

In Italy, the presence of the past inflected post-war architecture, not, as in the Fascist period, by classical references, but through a desire to fit into the historical urban fabric and enrich the limited language of technology-based Modernism from what was around. BBPR were a leading Milan firm who often outraged the movement's guardians but now seem to have been ahead of the trend of seeking to reinforce the particular character of places. The Torre Velasca, sited away from the main streets, is the antitype of the Seagram Building.

Säynätsalo Town Hall, Finland, 1949–51
—
Alvar Aalto (1898–1976)

In this small, remote building Aalto was a jump ahead of most of his contemporaries in understanding how to use a single material – red brick – shaped to reveal the identity of different parts of the building and composed so as to suggest a building with deep historical roots, especially in the case of the steps rising to a podium enclosed by buildings. His ingenuity extended into every detail, risking sentimentality but avoiding it with a sense of the appropriate. Many aspects of this project were imitated by Aalto's disciples, but never improved upon.

Housing at Gyttorp, Sweden, 1945–50
—
Ralph Erskine (1914–2005)

Gyttorp was the home of Alfred Nobel's explosives factory, Nitroglycerin AB, which commissioned a new housing district from Ralph Erskine at the end of World War II. Born and trained in England, the pacifist Erskine was in Sweden at the outbreak of war and decided to remain. His housing was built of lightweight concrete, using the strong colours that became a signature in his work, with lightweight concrete to make the wavy roof shapes. The houses were criticized for not conforming to Swedish tradition.

Busaras, Store Street, Dublin, 1944–53

—

Michael Scott (1905–89)

—

By the time that this major civic building – a bus station and offices combined – arose in Dublin, Michael Scott, whose earlier career included stage acting, had established a prominent position in Ireland, independent since 1922. He brought together a talented team and gave the rather backward country a joyous exercise with this wavy concrete canopy, engineered by Ove Arup, who set up a Dublin office, and many colourful decorations fulfilling the idea of 'la synthèse des arts' promoted by Le Corbusier.

Landscaping of the Acropolis and Philopappos Hill area, Athens, 1954–57

—

Dimitris Pikionis (1887–1968)

—

The postwar years saw the rise of landscape architecture as a means of defending the quality of places from the sameness of Modernism. The effect of 'groundscape' in the spaces between buildings became a theme of special interest. Pikionis sought to reinterpret ancient and Byzantine themes in his buildings from the 1920s onwards, but he is remembered above all for this work. A contemporary wrote, 'He was talking about us, but at the same time talking in the name of the people of the whole earth.'

**Apartments, Calle Bach,
Barceloneta, Catalonia, 1958**
—
**José Antonio Coderch i de
Sentmenat (1913–84)**
—
Spain during the Franco years
is often written out of the history
of Modernism, with the exception
of this remarkable building whose
faceted walls with sun screens
hide unusual trapezoid-plan rooms,
often leading on to screened
balconies. The recessed base
and the projecting eaves give the
building a traditional civic look.
Coderch continued to work in
Barcelona until 1978, the date
of his wavy-walled extension
to the architecture school.

138

Church of San Francesco d'Assisi al Fopponino, Via Paolo Giovio, Milan, 1961–64

—

Giò Ponti (1891–1979)

—

Magazine editor (*Domus*), product designer and architect, Ponti was an independent figure in post-war Italy, separated from the intellectual and political mainstream, enjoying his own formal invention with a deep concern for the feeling of being in his buildings. It is typical of his approach that this church facade forms the centrepiece of a theatrical grouping, flanked by two other related buildings, with screen walls repeating the diamond window shapes (echoing the plan form of Ponti's famous Pirelli Tower in Milan) through which one sees the sky.

**Balfron Tower, Brownfield Estate,
Tower Hamlets, London, 1965–67**
—
Ernö Goldfinger (1902–87)
—
Goldfinger, like Pouillon (see
opposite), was a disciple of Perret.
In older age, at a time when the
government in Britain saw towers
as a cheap form of housing, he had
the opportunity to build the tall
housing blocks he had imagined in
the 1930s. Goldfinger ensured that
the construction, in poured concrete,
was of high quality. Balfron Tower
forms a barrier against a tunnel
approach road, opening mainly
to the west. It takes its place as
part of a dynamic sculptural
grouping of lower blocks, with
green spaces enclosed. Following
this commission, Goldfinger built
Trellick Tower to a similar design
in North Kensington.

El Madania district, Algiers, 1954

—

Fernand Pouillon (1912–86)

—

Pouillon was a controversial figure
in French architecture – a prolific
builder of housing projects, mainly
for the lower middle classes around
Paris, but also in Marseilles, his
city of origin, and in Algiers in the
last years of French colonial rule.
He had 18 years of practice before
he took his diploma, and blurred
the lines between architect and
contractor. In addition, he made his
name as author of a history of the
medieval abbey of Le Thoronet, and
a memoir of his life, which included
a prison escape. He used structural
stone blocks even when building
cheap housing, giving his work
a traditional feel.

John Hancock Tower (now 200 Clarendon), Clarendon Place, Boston, Massachusetts, 1968–76

—

Henry N. Cobb (b.1926) of I.M. Pei (b.1917) and Partners

—

Ioeh Ming Pei (b.1917) was born in China but studied at MIT and taught at Harvard, where Henry Cobb was a student. They joined forces in 1955 and designed major corporate, government and museum buildings representing a mainstream of post-war Modernism. The Hancock Tower varied the Miesian model by being fully clad in reflective blue-tone glass with no distinct spandrel panels. The footprint is a parallelogram with deep insets on the short faces, so that the appearance changes according to the angle of vision. The construction was plagued by problems of stability and falling glass, contributing to the anti-Modernist mood of the late 1970s.

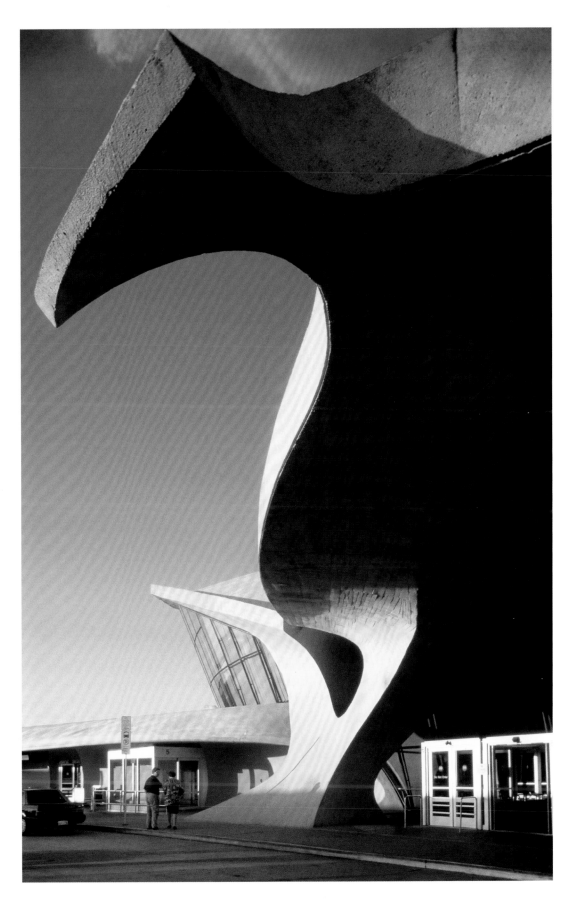

TWA Flight Center, John F. Kennedy International Airport, New York, 1955–62

—

Eero Saarinen (1910–61)

—

The son of Eliel Saarinen developed the 'organic' version of Modernism, with curves, as a recurrent although not universal theme in his short career, taken to its greatest extreme at the TWA terminal. The shape suggests metaphors of flight and was effective publicity while also providing efficient circulation, despite malfunctioning moving pavements. As Martin Pawley wrote, 'Saarinen really seemed to have caught up with satellites, jetliners, gas-turbine cars and the whole technological zeitgeist. Unhappily the triumph was – in part at least – illusory.'

Sydney Opera House, Bennelong Point, Sydney Harbour, 1957–73

—

Jørn Utzon (1918–2008), with engineers Arup (Ove Arup, 1895–1988)

—

The young Danish architect's sensational competition win (picked from the discard pile by Eero Saarinen) generated high expectations that tested technology beyond its limits in a botched procurement process owing to political pressure. The concept was a geometric one of segments of a sphere, making roofs for a larger and smaller auditorium. A philistine prime minister forced Utzon's resignation in 1966, and the interiors were not authentic. Only in 2004 did a reconciliation occur. Utzon's other work is of a markedly different character.

Berlin Philharmonie, 1956–63

—

Hans Scharoun (1893–1972)

—

Scharoun survived in Germany to enjoy a creative post-war career, including the Philharmonie and the library in the new Kulturforum, close to the line of the Berlin Wall. His competition design for the Philharmonie, placing the orchestra in the middle of 'vine terraces' of seating, beneath the convex curves of the roof, was judged by the conductor Herbert von Karajan to be acoustically excellent and suitable to the resident orchestra's style. The many stairs and routes to the seating through the auditorium provide a spectacle during intervals and make wayfinding surprisingly easy.

Beineke Rare Book and Manuscript Library, Yale University, New Haven, Connecticut, 1963

—

Skidmore, Owings and Merrill (Gordon Bunshaft, 1909–90)

—

Founded in 1936, SOM grew through military commissions and emerged with Lever House, New York, 1952, as innovative designers, not constrained by their anonymous group ethic, working in New York, Chicago and San Francisco. Their best-known work is commercial, but with the Beineke Library, Gordon Bunshaft of the New York office produced an innovative plan that made the books the chief visual event, housed in a glazed tower in the middle of a spacious hall lit through sheets of marble. The exterior shell stands on only four corner supports.

146

Yale University Art Gallery, New Haven, Connecticut, 1951–53

—

Louis Kahn (1901–74)

—

Kahn's study visit to Rome in 1950 transformed his architecture. Henceforth, he dealt with massive and solid forms, claiming 'there is no such thing as modern since everything belongs to architecture that exists in architecture'. The gallery at Yale, where he was already teaching, inaugurated his new direction, with its three-foot-deep floor slabs with triangular coffering, and its cylindrical stairway, with a repeated triangular theme.

Louisiana, 13 Gammel Strandvej, Humlebaek, Denmark, 1956–58

—

Vilhelm Wohlert (1920–2007) and Jørgen Bo (1919–99)

—

This famous museum was founded by Knud W. Jensen, a food exporter whose business flourished after the war, who was also passionately involved in modern culture. He discovered the Louisiana estate north of Copenhagen in 1955 and chose the little-known Wohlert, who brought an enthusiasm for the San Francisco Bay Area style to his designs (with Jørgen Bo) for a connected sequence of single-storey pavilions, finely crafted but intended to act as a frame to the works of art and the gardens seen through the windows.

Royal College of Physicians, Regent's Park, London, 1960–64

—

Denys Lasdun (1914–2001)

—

Like Kahn, Lasdun believed that the expressive quality of architecture had not been fundamentally changed by Modernism, although its range had been expanded. His headquarters for a venerable medical institution combines functional and ceremonial uses, with a dramatic spatial journey through a double-height atrium with views on to the garden. The idea of interpenetrating volumes and continuous space has rarely been better demonstrated. The enclosed 'box' contains the 'Censors Room', a seventeenth-century panelled interior transported from the college's first building.

Fuente de los Amantes, Los Clubes, Mexico, 1966

—

Luis Barragán (1902–88)

—

The Mexican architect's fame grew in the last years of his life, when his blend of historical inspiration from Mediterranean gardens and courtyards combined with the abstract geometry of Modernism and touches of Surrealism began to reach a world weary of machine imagery and eager for a more dreamlike architecture. Coloured walls and water under bright sun dating from the 1950s and 1960s provide the most evocative images of his work.

Art and Architecture Building, Yale University, New Haven, Connecticut, 1958–63

—

Paul Rudolph (1918–97)

—

After wartime experience in naval shipyards, Rudolph was fascinated by construction. As a Harvard student, he rejected Gropius's belief that urban design should be left to planners. He stated that 'there is perhaps too much concern in architectural circles about peripheral matters and too little understanding of age-old concepts, such as fine proportions, how to get into a building, relationships of volume to volume, how to relate building to the ground, the sky and so forth.' His complex, rough-skinned Yale building is the antitype of the nearby Beineke Library (see page 146).

Pacific Science Center, Seattle, 1962

—

Minoru Yamasaki (1912–86)

—

Born in Seattle as a Japanese American, Yamasaki drew inspiration from travels in Asia and Europe in 1954, incorporating Gothic and other references into his designs, which included the twin towers of the World Trade Center, New York, and the Pruitt–Igoe housing project in St. Louis, dynamited in 1972. The Pacific Science Center, originating from the Seattle World's Fair, shows Yamasaki's typical tightly spaced elevational patterns, and his lack of concern about breaking Modernist rules of good taste.

Il Magistero, Urbino University, Italy, 1968–76
—
Giancarlo De Carlo (1919–2005)
—

De Carlo's connection with the unspoilt hill town in the Italian Marches extended from 1955 to 2001, when he worked mostly for the university, partly on new buildings and partly conversions of old ones. The Magistero is the arts faculty, inserted into the walls of an old convent. Its plan creates indoor streets and terraced gardens linking lecture rooms and other facilities with clarity yet informality.

Municipal Orphanage, Amsterdam, 1955–60
—
Aldo van Eyck (1918–99)
—
This is probably the only architecturally famous example of its building type. Van Eyck was a vociferous rebel within CIAM, forming part of the young dissident group Team 10, who wanted to give Modern architecture more soul. This 'mat building' was part of a new movement in Modernism to demonumentalize. With an inspired client, Frans van Meurs, van Eyck reconfigured the idea of an institution, using repeated domed roofs to create a flowing plan with repeating house units along a 'street', and attractive sitting and stopping places.

Siedlung Halen, near Berne, Switzerland, 1955–61
—
Atelier 5 (founded 1955)
—
While much post-war housing aimed for height and mass, the Siedlung Halen took its cue from Le Corbusier's Roq et Rob (see page 124), using a gentle south-facing slope to build 81 private houses in terraces, providing privacy with patio gardens, but also including communal facilities for sport and leisure. The immediate surroundings of the houses are free of car traffic. Other similar examples became popular, especially in England where Atelier 5 built St Bernard's, Croydon, a smaller version of the same idea.

154

Park Hill Flats, Sheffield, 1958–61
—
J. Lewis Womersley (1910–89), city architect, with Jack Lynn (1926–2013) and Ivor Smith (b.1926)
—
From the start of Modernism, architects dreamed of making housing more architecturally eloquent. Tired of disconnected slab blocks or towers, Lynn and Smith proposed to join up sections of duplex housing, accessed by broad 'street decks', making a continuous figure built into a hillside to replace slum housing. The idea had been current for some time, but achieved a spectacular realization, seen as a valid replacement for older shapes of community. Over time, the verdict was less favourable, but following protection, a radical refurbishment was begun in 2009.

Engineering Building, University of Leicester, 1959–63
—
James Stirling (1926–92) and James Gowan (1923–2015)
—
Consisting of a tower of offices with lecture rooms, linked to a lower workshop block, the brief for the project inspired Stirling and Gowan to create a building of worldwide significance, full of formal invention and delight, recapturing the energy of the early 1920s. It was part of a generational shift in Britain, sometimes called 'New Brutalism', a label that Stirling and Gowan firmly rejected.

The Economist Buildings, St James's Street, London, 1959–64
—
Alison Smithson (1928–1993) and Peter Smithson (1923–2003)
—

Motivated in part by the client's desire for a penthouse flat, and the question of distributing the remaining accommodation for a magazine, some flats and a bank on a square site bounded by three streets, the Smithsons, central figures both of New Brutalism and Team 10, found scope for thoughts on 'the spaces in between', making a public piazza and a pedestrian shortcut raised up from the street, the location for the opening sequence of Antonioni's *Blow-Up* (1966). The actual buildings are respectfully detailed in Portland stone and aluminium. After this early success, the careers of the architects faltered, and they made their impact more through writing and teaching.

**Yoyogi National Gymnasium,
Tokyo, 1961–64**
—
Kenzō Tange (1913–2005)
—

Tange was the leading
representative of Modern
architecture in post-war Japan
and, through his followers,
influential in the Metabolist
movement launched in 1960 that
imagined the city as a place of
continuous change. He was the
chief architect for the Tokyo
Olympics, the Gymnasium being
built for the occasion. It is based
on a spine cable from which are
hung curving concrete roofs,
split down the middle and
mirrored in shape, enclosing
a circular arena.

7
—
New
Fabrication
and New
Form
—
1920—
1975

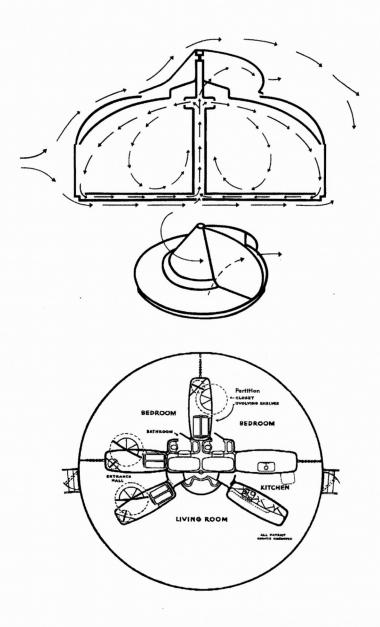

Wichita House, 1945–46

—

Richard Buckminster Fuller
(1895–1983)

—

Buckminster Fuller was an inventor and visionary who believed in the science-based transformation of ordinary living. Derived from his 1930 Dymaxion House project, the Wichita House aimed to harness aircraft production at the end of the war to create a cheap and efficient new form of housing. The upper diagram shows the principle of airflow in the house, the lower the plan with pivoting storage and bathroom 'pods'. However, Fuller's perfectionism held back production and the initiative was lost.

The mechanical dream of a rational, controlled, Cartesian world long pre-dated Modernism and its reality was glimpsed in the early factories of the industrial revolution. Modern architecture aimed to replace the intuitive forms of the pre-modern world by learning from new materials and creating new rational assembly processes by which they might become buildings. From these technical concerns, a new form of architectural expression appropriate for the Modern age would be born. As Le Corbusier wrote, 'Les techniques sont l'assiette même du lyrisme' (roughly translated, 'Techniques are the foundation of poetry'). In reality, the poetry often controlled the techniques, and Modernist history contains a string of famous but unwanted or unbuildable designs that are fantasies based on the idea of technology, while denying social and physical reality.

This chapter moves away from the world of conventional craft building to one based on patent applications, standardized components, and time and motion studies on the building site. Walter Gropius made two attempts to realize this dream of factory-made housing, neither of them produced in large numbers, in contrast to the multi-purpose arched Nissen hut, designed for the British Army in 1916. Buckminster Fuller invented devices to replace standard cars, boats and houses, based on ergonomic study. His Dymaxion House (1930) was designed for ease of delivery and assembly, with a bathroom installed as a single pod. Inspiring though these ideas were to later designers, only Fuller's faceted geodesic domes were built in any numbers, sometimes as 'alternative' dwellings, as at Drop City.

The conditions of shortage and an acute need for buildings after World War II stimulated experiments in prefabrication, including those of metalworker Jean Prouvé in France. On similar lines, the system devised in England for rapid construction of schools after 1945 fulfilled its aims at a time when conventional materials and skills were scarce. The team research and building exercises needed in the war inspired the collaborative ethos. The California Case Study Houses aimed for similar sharing of concepts, to make open-plan living accessible to all, but in reality it was products outside the sphere of Modern architecture that achieved success with the market.

Later came adaptations of heavyweight building to systematized assembly, with the pre-cast concrete pods of Moshe Safdie's 1967 Habitat at Montreal, and Kisho Kurokawa's Nagakin Capsule Tower Hotel, as well as the system-built housing favoured by 1960s governments as an economy, which mostly used concrete panels. Some engineers, notably Pier Luigi Nervi, took an architectural role in the design of wide-span concrete roofs with beautiful rib patterns, while others, such as Ove Arup, collaborated with architects to find new plan forms such as the 'tartan grid', whereby service zones alternated with the main spaces and were expressed externally. By contrast, Frei Otto pioneered lightweight fabric roofs under tension.

The modular design systems could be humanized in the projects to which they gave shape, including Herman Hertzberger's Centraal Beheer, where people took precedence, and in John Johansen's Mummers Theater, with its three pods linked like lunar modules.

Dymaxion House Model, 1928

Richard Buckminster Fuller (1895–1983)

In a long tradition of non-architectural creators of building ideas, Fuller took the analogy of a tree, with its mast-trunk at the centre, and lightweight translucent casein walls hung from cables. His model for production and updating was the car. The name was coined by the promotion manager of the Marshall Field store in Chicago, where the Dymaxion (a portmanteau of the words 'dynamic', 'maximum' and 'tension') house model was first exhibited.

162 **Nissen Hut, everywhere, 1916**

Peter Norman Nissen (1871–1930)

Nissen, an American-Canadian mining engineer, joined the British Expeditionary Force in 1914 and two years later invented his hut. The roof is made of corrugated iron sections supported on light T-section supports, with timber infill for the two ends. The design allowed for compact transportation and easy erection. There were 100,000 built during the 1914–18 war, and many again in 1939–45. They could be used for a variety of purposes, although only a few were adopted for long-term living accommodation. The success of the Nissen hut contrasts with the commercial failure of Fuller's prefabricated house projects.

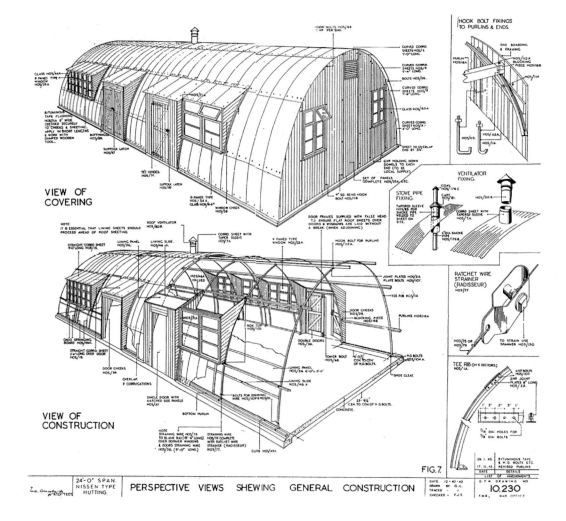

Biosphere, Montreal, 1965–67

—

**Richard Buckminster Fuller
(1895–1983)**

—

Fuller's faceted geodesic domes were his most successful building idea, built on all scales in a variety of materials. He was commissioned by the US government to build its pavilion for Expo 67, and made a three-quarter sphere with a diameter of 250 feet (76 metres), with a double skin of acrylic and a computer-operated sun-shading system. In 1976, a fire destroyed the acrylic, but the structure survived and was reopened in 1995 as an exhibition about water, climate change and related issues.

Schindler/Chace House, 835 N Kings Road, West Hollywood, California, 1921–22

—

Rudolph Schindler (1887–1953)

—

Schindler moved from Vienna to Chicago early in 1914, and worked for Frank Lloyd Wright in California, where he built a double house for his wife and himself, plus another couple, the Chaces. 'The distinction between indoors and outdoors will disappear', wrote Schindler. For the walls, he used concrete tilt-slab walls, cast flat on the ground and then pulled up into place, a technique pioneered in Califorinia by Irving Gill, which Schindler had practised when working with Wright. The houses have been preserved as a museum.

164 **Rosenbaum House, 601 Riverview Drive, Florence, Alabama, 1939–40**

—

Frank Lloyd Wright (1867–1959)

—

Wright's 'Usonian' houses were a middle way between the custom-built individual house and the standardized product. By specifying a common language of forms and materials, with certain assumptions about the L-shaped plan, with the kitchen at the hinge, the houses could then be adapted to the needs of particular clients and sites, and built relatively cheaply and quickly by Wright's apprentices from his Taliesin office-school, who arrived with a roll of drawings to supervise the work until it was completed. The houses offered an elegant solution to housing the cash-strapped middle classes in the Depression.

Maison du Peuple, Clichy, Paris, 1935–39

—

Eugène Beaudoin (1898–1983) and Marcel Lods (1891–1978), with Vladimir Bodiansky, engineer (1894–1966), and Jean Prouvé, steelwork fabricator (1901–84)

—

This is a revolutionary building in its construction, built by a left-wing suburban commune on the fringes of Paris. Jean Prouvé came from a metalworking family in Nancy and became an indispensible colleague for many architects because of his ability to provide novel components. At Clichy, he invented pressed steel panels as cladding, providing rigidity and insulated with a filling of glass wool. The floors and roof were retractable, allowing for varying use as a market and a community meeting hall.

Levittown, Hempstead, Long Island, New York, 1947–51
—
Levitt & Sons Inc. (Alfred Levitt, 1912–66, and William Levitt, 1907–94)
—
William Levitt, experienced in military building during the war, saw the business opportunity for developing a large community in the potato fields of Long Island, and got his architect brother Alfred to design a limited range of types that proved very popular. The sites were cleared of all existing features, and the original Levittown and its several successors became a byword for soulless subjugation to conventional attitudes. The physical production of effective low-cost housing outperformed any rival systems of greater architectural pretension.

Airstream 'Clipper' Caravan, 1936
—
Wallace Merle 'Wally' Byam (1896–1962)
—
As publisher of a do-it-yourself magazine, Wally Byam tried out a caravan design for himself and then introduced his own innovations – a dropped floor between the wheels and a higher ceiling. The success of his design led him into full-time production, with the Airstream name registered in 1931. The 'Clipper', with its semi-monocoque aluminium shell and side door, appeared five years later and is now a recognized design classic, offering constructional ideas for architecture.

Segal Close and Walters Way, Lewisham, South London, 1979–84

—

Walter Segal (1907–85)

—

The picture shows the German émigré architect Walter Segal greeting one of the self-builders who realized two separate schemes using his designs for timber houses in the early 1980s. Segal studied the idea of the simple house, and built his own prototype in 1963 before the self-build approach became seen as an opportunity to empower residents in future communities, making use of land too steep for conventional construction. The project brought back some of the anarchist self-help initiative lost in the mass production of post-war housing.

Drop City, Trinidad, Colorado, 1965–73

—

Gene Bernofsky (b.1941), Jo Ann Bernofsky (b.1942), Richard Kallweit (b.1943) and Clark Richert (b.1941)

—

The three founders of Drop City were students at the University of Kansas, inspired by 'Happenings' and by John Cage, Robert Rauschenberg and Richard Buckminster Fuller, whose dome shapes provided the inspiration for homes in the original hippy commune on land they bought for the purpose. With no building experience, they used a variety of recycled materials, including bottle tops and sheet steel from car bodies. The utopian vision, clouded by the arrival of unwanted visitors, lasted just eight years.

Prefabricated housing, Route des Gardes, Meudon, Paris, 1950

—

Jean Prouvé (1901–84), with Henri Prouvé (1915–2012) and André Sive (1899–1958)

—

Fourteen surplus prefab houses, originally ordered by Housing Minister Claudius Petit but not used, found their way from Prouvé's workshop in Nancy to the southwest suburbs of Paris. The folded steel components can be assembled without any lifting equipment, with a modified portal frame truss and cladding panels for roof and walls. The interior can be flexibly configured. The houses are raised off the ground on steel supports, although most have masonry infilling.

**Margaret Wix Primary School,
St Albans, Hertfordshire,
England, 1956**

—

**Architects Co-Partnership
(founded 1939)**

—

Hertfordshire County Council pioneered a prefabricated lightweight steel building system for schools in the 1940s, linked to a child-centred design approach, with generous space, clear, bright colours and informal planning. It was a solution to the shortage of conventional materials and building skills afer the war, and a fulfilment of the Modernist aim of rationalizing building components and assembly procedures. Independent architects, such as ACP, were hired to help meet the demand for school places among the baby boomers, and made use of the system.

Cité de la Muette, Drancy, Seine-Saint-Denis, France, 1930–34

—

**Eugène Beaudoin (1898–1983)
and Marcel Lods (1891–1978),
with engineer Eugène Mopin
(dates unknown)**

—

Using a lightweight steel-frame construction system developed by Mopin, and doors and windows by Jean Prouvé, the 15-storey tower blocks of housing were erected first, with lower-rise housing spreading out below them. Social and sporting amenities were cut in the financial crisis of the early 1930s, and the tower flats were hard to let, so the complex was turned over to military use in 1938, before becoming a notorious internment and transit station for concentration camps during the war. The towers were demolished in 1976.

170

Spa Green Flats, Islington, London, 1945–49

—

Berthold Lubetkin (1901–90) and Tecton (founded 1932), with engineer Ove Arup (1895–1988) and Peter Dunican (1918–89). Illustration by Margaret Potter (1916–97)

—

A breakthrough was made in concrete construction in Britain when the 'box frame' devised by Ove Arup was permitted, using prefabricated concrete wall and floor slabs rather than conventional slabs, and more expensive and visually intrusive columns and beams. Lubetkin grasped the expressive possibilities of the brick infill on the elevations as a medium for pattern-making.

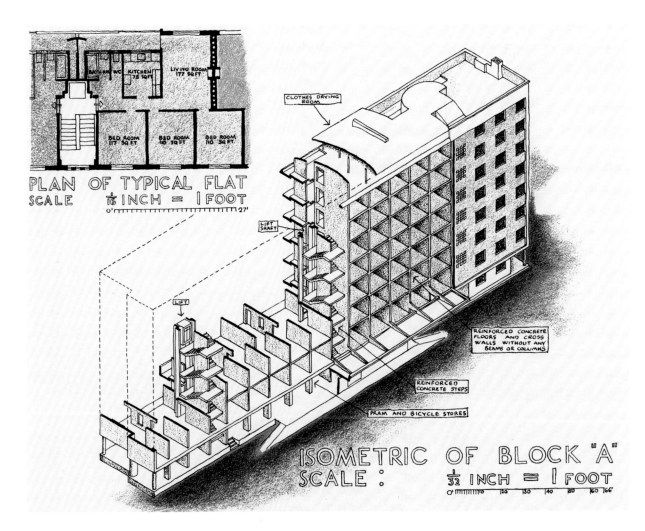

PLAN OF TYPICAL FLAT
SCALE ¹⁄₁₆ INCH = 1 FOOT

ISOMETRIC OF BLOCK "A"
SCALE : ¹⁄₃₂ INCH = 1 FOOT

Habitat 67, Montreal, 1967

—

Moshe Safdie (b.1938)

—

Canada's Expo 67 caught the world at the peak of post-war technological optimism, and Habitat 67, by an architect still under 30, demonstrated how housing might be transformed by factory production of three-dimensional stackable units, which had been the subject of Safdie's final-year thesis at McGill University. Lego bricks, then beginning their international ascent, were used for design models. Apart from the construction novelty, which was not directly carried forward, Habitat 67 aimed to provide community and a degree of privacy with open space for each unit.

9 Ash Street, Cambridge, Massachusetts, 1941–42

—

Philip Johnson (1906–2005)

—

After curating the MoMA 'Modern Architecture: International Exhibition' in 1932, Philip Johnson travelled in Europe and became involved in Fascist politics. During the war, he enrolled in the Graduate School of Design at Harvard and could afford to build a simple house nearby as a thesis study, using plywood walls. The idea of constructional simplicity, inherited from the American building tradition, was an important aspect of Modernism's acclimatization in the USA, and the departure from the standard suburban-lot layout challenged convention. The house is now owned by Harvard University.

Bailey House (Case Study House No.21), 9038 Wonderland Park Avenue, Los Angeles, 1958

—

Pierre Koenig (1925–2004)

—

John Entenza's Case Study House programme ran from 1945–62, using *Arts & Architecture* magazine as a platform for promoting new ideas for houses at the middle range of cost. All were in California. Koenig studied under Richard Neutra and, like most other case study architects, worked in steel, which provided a sense of discipline at a time when bad taste had become almost a national principle. This house uses a 22-foot (6.7-metre) module, made off site, to achieve spacious openings and accuracy for fitting windows. Seductive images of this house, and others like it, travelled widely.

174

Air Force Hangar, Orvieto, Italy, 1935

—

Pier Luigi Nervi (1891–1979) and Giovanni Bartoli (1932–57)

—

Acting as designer and contractor, Nervi won this competition with his cousin, Bartoli, with an efficient structure that was nonetheless expensive in its need for an all-in-one concrete pouring with a massive amount of shuttering. The result fulfilled the Modernist hope that perfect structures might resemble natural forms. This and later hangers were destroyed by retreating Germans during the war, but Nervi's career continued with more spectacular ribbed roofs.

Mining and Metallurgy Building, University of Birmingham, 1966

—

Arup Associates (Sir Philip Dowson, 1924–2014, and Ronald Hobbs, 1923–2006)

—

The engineering consultancy Ove Arup & Partners (now Arup) decided to set up an architectural practice in 1963, often working for higher education and industry and more than usually interested in the ventilation needed for research environments. The Birmingham University building pioneered the use of a 'tartan grid', so named because of the alternation of wide and narrow zones. In the latter, piping, wiring and ducts could be neatly inserted and made easily accessible for maintenance. The rhythm also gave the building its character.

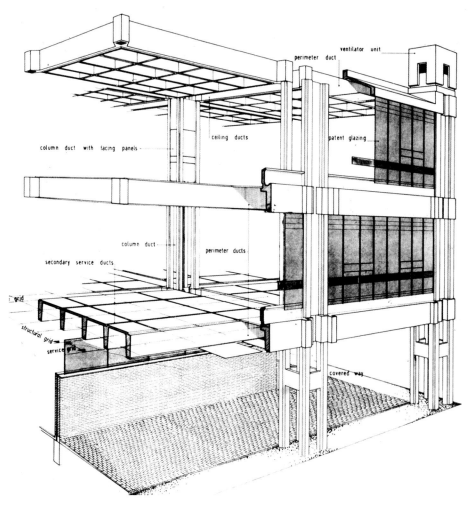

Munich Olympic Stadium, 1968–72

—

Frei Otto (1925–2015) and Günther Behnisch (1922–2010)

—

From childhood onwards, Frei Otto was involved in activities involving various kinds of membrane structures, an idea whose time arrived in the 1960s, with collaboration with biologists and mathematicians, textile manufacturers and architects, developed through proposals for dams, suspended reservoirs and pneumatic structures. These were often conceived for large public events, the most famous being the Munich Olympic Stadium.

Centraal Beheer, Apeldoorn, The Netherlands, 1967–72
—
Herman Hertzberger (b.1932)
—
Like several of his Dutch contemporaries, among them Aldo van Eyck, Hertzberger was opposed to the soulless and mechanical development of cities. He produced his alternative at Apeldoorn, where an insurance building for over 1,000 workers was designed to give a sense of individuality to separate clusters of relatively small spaces, lit by cruciform internal atria. The intention was achieved partly because company policy encouraged personalization of the separate pods.

Mummers Theater, Oklahoma City, 1970
—
John Johansen (1916–2012)
—
After studying at Harvard under Walter Gropius (whose adopted daughter he married), Johansen became increasingly interested in de-monumentalizing larger buildings by breaking them down into visibly different components. The Mummers Theater, winner of an award in 1972, exemplified this tendency, but was demolished in 2014. In later life, Johansen became interested in the possibility of holistic architecture, where 'all functions, services, structures, equipment and aesthetic effects [are] designed as an inseparable whole'.

178

Nagakin Capsule Tower Hotel, Shimbashi, Tokyo, 1972

—

Kisho Kurokawa (1934–2007)

—

One of the founders of Metabolism, Kurokawa aimed to avoid permanence as a non-Japanese value, and to express flux and change. The total transformation of cities was never achievable, but the Nagakin Capsule Tower is a suggestive fragment, using the idea of plug-in minimal rooms attached to a service core, riding above the city expressway. The building became obsolescent and half empty. Demolition has been threatened, but so far held off.

Olivetti Training Centre (now Branksome Conference Centre), Haslemere, England, 1969–72
—
James Stirling (1926–92)
—
Moving on from the use of red brick, Stirling chose glass-reinforced polyester (GRP) panels for this remarkable *Avengers*-style extension to an Edwardian country house. He wanted alternating violet and lime green panels but, although the building is remote from other houses, was forced to tone down the colour. The panels were meant to 'click into place' but film footage shows workmen hitting them with sledgehammers.

Futuro House, 1968–70, displayed at Marché Dauphine, Saint-Ouen, Paris since 2013
—
Matti Suuronen (1933–2013)
—
This Finnish architect devoted his career to designing in plastics of various kinds, producing two house types, the circular Futuro and the square Venturo, with wider openings. The UFO-shaped Futuro was composed of 16 GRP panels on a steel support and could be bought as a kit to erect on site. It was designed with use as a ski lodge in mind, because it could be placed on any terrain and would warm up quickly. Examples were sold around the world but it never achieved large numbers.

8
—
Recovered Memory
—
1950–2000

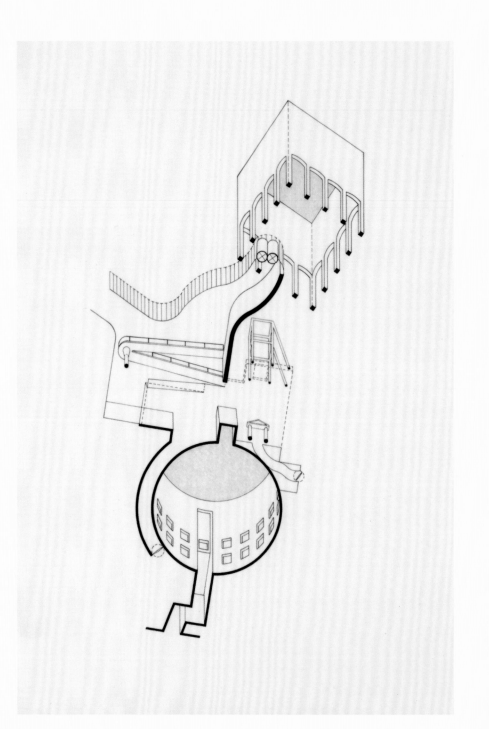

This unbuilt scheme was a turning point for Stirling, moving him towards cultural buildings with classical references. The drawing isolates the new-build elements, but their oddity was the result of threading them through existing buildings in the heart of the city to create an exciting route with an exterior gathering place (the portico at the top of the drawing). Stirling enjoyed the 'worm's eye' axonometric for its surprising and vivid way of explaining spaces.

We are used to defining architecture in the twentieth century in terms of the *tabula rasa* from which traces of the past have been wiped. Such were the ambitions of some of the century's most tyrannical rulers, while others infected classical forms with undesirable associations for many years to come. The desire to 'make it new' could, however, include the reworking of the past, as was the case with the poetry of Ezra Pound, who famously gave this command.

The context of building in historic cities in the post-war decades became an incentive to choosing materials and composing with forms at a scale commensurate with the fine grain of older buildings. This was, not surprisingly, an area in which Italian architects excelled. From such early and controversial infill buildings as Gardella's House on the Zattere in Venice, the permission to play with the past was accorded to Carlo Scarpa's original interventions at Verona, while the Neo-Rationalists of the 1970s such as Aldo Rossi let the character of cities and their components take precedence over the 'needs' of traffic. Port Grimaud, a 1960s French holiday village and marina, rattled the certainties of Modernism because it felt as good as a historic place, and so the doors began to open on what became 'Postmodernism', a term developed to describe a more general literary and cultural relativism and self-awareness, which had always been Modernism's shadow side, and which appeared in architectural literature at intervals from the 1940s before the critic Charles Jencks named it as a movement in 1977.

Robert Venturi was one of the leaders, with his short book *Complexity and Contradiction in Architecture* (1966), a manifesto for double meaning and sly fun, while Charles Moore explored the sensory side of dwelling and the evocation of ancient forms. James Stirling, once the apostle of technical innovation, and Philip Johnson, the high priest of Miesian minimalism, both embraced new opportunities to enrich their designs with jokes and references to the past. Initially, this movement could be irritating and self-regarding, but the longer-term effect on saving the texture of historic cities and considering the emotional needs of building users has been wholly beneficial, especially in the design of housing, and it is now impossible to write a convincing history of Modernism that does not give full attention to Postmodernism. While it was imagined as an opposition, it is arguably more deeply rooted in the original movement, something that has been obscured from view on account of the early histories that deliberately excised anything that showed signs of decoration, stylistic memory or gratuitous expression. Perhaps as the theorist Jean-François Lyotard explained in 1979, 'A work can become modern only if it is first postmodern. Postmodernism thus understood is not modernism at its end but in the nascent state, and this state is constant.' Thus, the 'Postmodern Condition' (the title of the book in which this conclusion was reached) was not a perversion of the post-war years, but inherent in the whole project.

House on the Zattere, Venice, 1954–58

—

Ignazio Gardella (1905–99)

—

A new building on a conspicuous site in Venice required tact, and Gardella succeeded in updating the Venetian palazzo without literalism. Reyner Banham wrote, 'The building's most conspicuous virtue is to look like a conversion job at first sight, and then reveal somewhere between second and seventh sight that it is basically a masterpiece of the stylist's art. … I am convinced there is an extremely important lesson to be learned here.'

184 **Frog Meadow, Dedham, Essex, England, 1967, 1969 and 1972**

—

Raymond Erith (1904–73)

—

These simple village houses are meant to look as if they have grown up over time. Erith resisted Modernism but thought deeply about how classicism could be justified as part of a spectrum of design growing out of vernacular building practice. After his death, he was recognized as an original thinker and much more than a pasticheur. Although often witty, his architecture was never ironic. The row of buildings was later extended by Quinlan Terry (b.1937) who continued Erith's practice.

US Embassy, New Delhi, 1954
—
Edward Durrell Stone (1902–78)
—

Stone's first independent work was the Museum of Modern Art in New York (with Philip Goodwin), 1938, but he went on to develop a more historically conscious and decorative approach, reverting to his pre-Modernist training. This turn alienated the purists, but Stone was recognized by anti-Modernist writers such as Tom Wolfe as an important early rebel against what he saw as an alien European puritanical taste at odds with American consumerism.

Promontory Point, Sea Ranch, Sonoma County, California, 1964–72
—
Masterplanner and landscape architect Lawrence Halprin (1916–2009); architects MLTW (Charles Moore, 1925–93, Donlyn Lyndon, b.1936, William Turnbull, 1935–77, and Richard Whitaker, b.1929)
—
The developer Alfred Boeke saw the Sea Ranch site from a plane and picked a team of young architects to work in a unified manner in a carefully restored landscape to make a second-home settlement. Local farm buildings provided the inspiration for shapes and materials, and Mediterranean island villages for the clustered form – 'a choreography of the familiar and the surprising'. Moore was an influential thinker and teacher who embraced the whole of history to make architecture more emotionally appealing.

**Port Grimaud, Var, France,
1966–69**
—
François Spoerry (1912–99)
—
For this holiday village, the
Resistance fighter and Dachau
internee Spoerry opened up to the
pleasures of life, basing his plan
on the exclusion of cars and access
to boat moorings from most of the
houses. The choice of a Provençal
vernacular was appropriate and,
while shocking for some, exercised
fascination among commentators
such as Peter and Alison Smithson
who were beginning to question
the assumptions of Modernism.

Quincy Market Development, Boston, Massachusetts, 1824–26, converted 1976
—
Alexander Parris (1780–1852); conversion by Benjamin Thompson (1918–2002) and Associates
—
Between the waterfront and the historic city, the robust neoclassical market in the Faneuil Hall area of Boston was abandoned in the late 1960s. The retail developer James Rouse worked with Benjamin Thompson, who already had a record in building conservation, to convert the protected market and its surroundings into one of the first so-called 'festival marketplaces', recognized as a new approach to inner-city regeneration serving a local population and tourists alike with unusual shops and restaurants.

Schullin Jewellery Shop II, Kohlmarkt, Vienna, 1981–82
—
Hans Hollein (1934–2014)
—
Austrian architects between the wars were critical of the more dogmatic precepts of CIAM. Hollein studied art in Vienna, and then architecture in the USA with Mies van der Rohe, from whom he acquired an interest in new materials, while also being influenced by early 1960s artistic culture to believe that 'everything is architecture', practising from the scale of city planner to product designer. His shops challenged the dour assumptions within Modernism, and Charles Jencks wrote that 'so much design talent and mystery expended on such small shops would convince an outsider that he had at last stumbled on the true faith of this civilization'.

Clos Pegase Winery, Napa Valley, California, 1984–87

—

Michael Graves (1934–2015)

—

Graves formed part of a teaching group at Princeton in the 1960s and '70s, concerned with alternatives to the 'official style' of American Modernism. In 1972, following a series of conferences at MoMA and elsewhere, he was featured with some of these in a book titled *Five Architects*, performing complex mannerist manipulations on the works of the 1920s masters, as weekend homes for artistic clients. From this position, he worked his way to become one of the defining figures of Postmodernism. His winery epitomizes the movement's contradictory qualities: leisure industry, democratic elitism and a contemporary past.

Conversion of Museo Civico di Castelvecchio, Verona, 1959–73
—
Carlo Scarpa (1906–78)
—
Scarpa's work with old buildings began in 1937, when he reworked the interiors of Ca' Foscari in his native Venice for the university there. In the same year, he began to design exhibitions, and gained contacts in the museum world, being commissioned in 1957 to work on the fourteenth-century Castelvecchio. Scarpa established a route through the building, with objects carefully placed to look good in themselves and in relationship, including the dramatic emergence into an open void in the building.

Kimbell Art Museum, Fort Worth, Texas, 1966–72
—
Louis Kahn (1901–74)
—
One of Kahn's last buildings, the Kimbell was planned with separate gallery spaces as a reaction against the open-plan Yale Art Gallery (see page 148). Kahn also wanted natural lighting to 'give the comforting feeling of knowing the time of day' and this comes from skylights in curved concrete vaults, passing across diffusers. The same vault shape extends into the exterior to act as a welcome to visitors from the park in which the museum stands.

190

—

**James Stirling (1926–92)
and Michael Wilford (b.1938)**

—

A local official explained the commissioning of this building, Stirling's breakthrough after some wilderness years, saying, 'He has set impulses to architecture which have not been received during the last 20 years.' Adding to an existing U-shaped museum, Stirling transcribed the classical original into fragmented but still legible forms, creating a public footpath through the drum-shaped void of the central sculpture court, behind the formal games of the entrance.

Interior conversion of the Musée d'Orsay, Paris, 1981–86

—

Gae Aulenti (1927–2012)

—

The Beaux-Arts railway station on the Left Bank was due for demolition in 1970 but protests saved it and instead it was proposed to act as a new museum of nineteenth-century art, one of François Mitterand's 'Grands Projets'. Gae(tana) Aulenti worked in the 1950s in the controversial 'Neo-Liberty' manner that reflected Art Nouveau. Her sympathy for this period is implicit rather than explicit in the adaptation of the echoing single-vault space, with smaller galleries to each side.

Museo Nacional de Arte Romano, Mérida, Spain, 1980–86

—

Rafael Moneo (b.1937)

—

After the death of Francisco Franco in 1975, Spain experienced rapid cultural development and decentralization. The museum at Mérida was one of the results. It is built over the top of remains of the Roman town and close to its surviving theatre and amphitheatre. The bricks are long and thin in Roman style, and the main basilical hall of the museum makes a strong allusion to this past, as if it sits in the stripped shell of an ancient building.

192

The Garden Temple, Little Sparta, Dunsyre, Scotland, 1982

—

Ian Hamilton Finlay (1925–2006)

—

Finlay, a visual poet, moved with his wife, Sue, to a remote small farm in southern Scotland in 1966 and started work on the garden, which was a test bed for putting words and ideas in physical form in landscape. Themes of boats and the sea, and of modern war, were joined by classical deities and references to European culture of the Romantic period, especially of the French Revolution, as reminders of the continuity of both growth and death. Apollo's temple, converted from a former farm building, exemplifies the garden's marriage of the everyday and the sublime.

Museum of Decorative Arts, Frankfurt, 1979–85

—

Richard Meier (b.1934)

—

With Michael Graves (see page 189), Meier was one of the 'New York Five' and has remained true to the whiteness of their early work. His contribution to the museum area in Frankfurt is a highly mannered elaboration of the square plan of the small 1830s villa already existing on the site, which is linked by a bridge to the rest of the complex. Here there is an attractive play of light and space, with a sense of enclosed but essentially 'outdoor' circulation, calculated using two intersecting grids.

194

San Cataldo Cemetery, Modena, Italy, 1971–78

—

Aldo Rossi (1931–97)

—

Rossi's book *The Architecture of the City* (1966) marks a turning point in thinking, away from the functional and instrumental understanding of the city, and from its antithesis, the picturesque city, whether conceived historically or futuristically. Instead, the city is seen, in very European terms, as something with its own history and character (described as typology) that is beyond rationality yet vital to any proper way of living. After the failed revolutions of 1968, this limited, Stoic outlook prevailed and was taken up by the left. The San Cataldo cemetery extension, designed as a huge cloistered ossuary, is both highly intellectual and unquestionably emotional.

194

198

Mosque of Rome, Parioli, Rome, 1974–95

—

Paolo Portoghesi (b.1931), engineer Vittorio Gigliotti (b.1921) and Sami Mousawi (b.1938)

—

Portoghesi is a key figure in the many-sided development of architecture after Modernism, teaching, writing, editing and curating the first architectural exhibition at the Venice Biennale, 'The Presence of the Past', in 1981. His catalogue essay was titled 'The End of Prohibitionism' and declared that the attempt to suppress historical memory had been defeated by 'the human condition'. The mosque responds to the very different perceptions of time and the meaning of change in Islam, using curvaceous concrete columns suggestive of Art Nouveau.

**Corniche Mosque, Jeddah,
Saudi Arabia, 1986**
—
Abdel-Wahid El-Wakil (b.1943)
—
El-Wakil was educated in Egypt
in an English school (where he
discovered Ruskin) and took a
normal Modernist architectural
course, but turned against his
training and discovered the work
of Hassan Fathy (1900–89), using
traditional materials and forms,
and took these as his guide. His
mosques from the 1980s have
a simplicity and purity not often
found, and he has also built
traditional city courtyard houses.
He was architect for the Oxford
Centre for Islamic Studies, built
of loadbearing materials.

Houses at Mexicali, Mexico, 1975–76

—

Christopher Alexander (b.1936)

—

Christopher Alexander moved from mathematically based architectural theory to an engagement with people as builders. The Mexicali project provided a simple improvised building method using concrete, while encouraging residents to find self-expression through following a code. The rationale and the outcomes were recorded in *The Production of Houses* (1985), one of the many books that Alexander and his colleagues have written, developing an alternative theory of architecture and design that is neither historical nor Modern in the conventional sense.

Social housing, Ritterstrasse, Kreuzberg, Berlin, 1980–83

—

Rob Krier (b.1938)

—

Rob Krier and his brother Léon have been important urban theorists since the mid-1970s, when they proposed radical alternatives to Modernist city planning, based on the idea of typologies, often illustrated by simplified neoclassical buildings. Rob Krier was given the opportunity to build using a modified version of traditional German courtyard housing as part of the Internationale Bauausstellung (IBA) held through the mid-1980s, with medium-rise apartments linked by pedestrian paths. These were in contrast to the 1957 IBA at Hansaviertel, consisting of housing blocks standing in isolation among grass and trees.

**AT&T Building (now Sony Tower),
550 Madison Avenue, New York,
1979–84**
—
**Philip Johnson (1906–2005)
and John Burgee (b.1933)**
—
Having been one of Modernism's
earliest supporters in the USA,
Johnson was a restless figure and
propelled new movements in his
old age, including a developing
sense of the specific qualities
of American archecture. The
'Chippendale' skyscraper was his
most notorious design, playing up
to Robert Venturi's promotion of
the 'billboard' facade of 'decorated
shed' as a means of identification.

202

Clinical Research Building, University of Pennsylvania, 1988–90

—

Robert Venturi (b.1925) and Denise Scott Brown (b.1931)

—

Venturi's book *Complexity and Contradiction in Architecture* (1966) is the most readable Postmodernist text, presenting a strong and wittily argued case for enrichment of form and meaning in buildings. With Denise Scott Brown, he has practised in his birthplace, Philadelphia, since 1960. Their Clinical Research Building echoes the campus style in its variegated brickwork and adds a typical 'decorated shed' touch with the coat of arms.

National Theatre of Catalonia, Barcelona, 1991–97

—

Ricardo Bofill (b.1939), Taller del Arquitectura (founded 1963)

—

In 1974, after several years of practice in Spain, Bofill won the competition for the site of Les Halles in central Paris. He did not carry out the work in the end, but did continue to work in Paris, building massive theatrical housing blocks in the suburbs, using giant classical elements. To design a theatre later on was perhaps appropriate, and the temple shape with rows of 'incorrect' columns recalls the 1980s at a time when such elements were falling out of favour. In his heyday, Bofill was considered a major figure.

9
—
Landscape and Location
—
1965– 2014

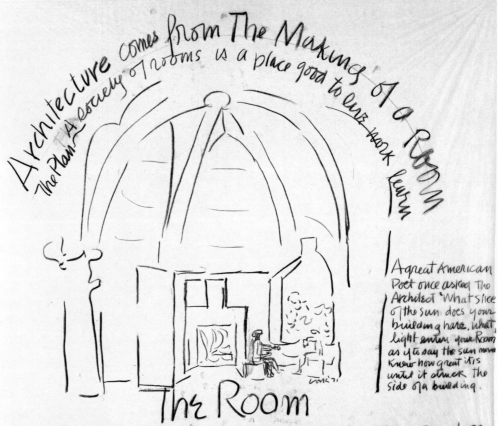

Architecture comes from The Making of a Room
The Plan A society of rooms is a place good to live. Work learn — Louis Kahn

A great American Poet once asked the Architect 'What slice of the sun does your building have. what light enters your Room as if to say the sun never knew how great it is until it struck the side of a building.

The Room

is The place of the mind. In a small room one does not say what one would in a large room In a room with only one other person could be generative The vectors of each meet. A room is not a room without natural light. natural light gives the time of day and the mood of the seasons to enter.

Kahn's graphic meditation on
enclosure and sunlight exemplifies
an influential if unexpected direction
in architecture at the end of the 1960s,
when a public display of subjective
feeling, often rather portentously
delivered, served as an antidote to
the materialistic character of the age.
Kahn's architecture carried authority
and his teaching transmitted the new
way of presenting architecture.

In synchrony with the more historically based Postmodernism came an alternative humanizing strand within the Modern movement, based on the concept of place – especially the rural or natural setting for a building. This is often identified with the philosophical tradition of phenomenology and its resistance to scientific positivism, and particularly the writings of Martin Heidegger, which revive the idea of a mystical relationship between man and the earth and heavens. Throughout the development of Modernism, some architects have always inserted their buildings sensitively into the landscape, with echoes of materials won from the earth and the forms of anonymous folk building. Not surprisingly, such buildings appeal to deep-rooted emotions and become sites of architectural pilgrimage, like Carlo Scarpa's extraordinary little village cemetery at Brion.

Sometimes it has been the products of the land that have contributed to shaping the buildings: stones for the Thermal Baths at Vals, or green oak for Edward Cullinan's Downland Gridshell. Northern European countries are especially associated with this tendency. Alvar Aalto never lost sight of his childhood experience as the son of a forester in Finland, and was followed by two younger Nordic masters – Sverre Fehn in Norway, and Jorn Utzøn in Denmark – yet it required a Catalan, Enric Miralles, to capture the essence of Scotland in the new Parliament building in Edinburgh. Here, as in Lucien Kroll's work at Louvain University, the irregularity of the building deliberately evokes the processes that create form in nature.

Churches, where light is the expressive medium, belong in this category, with Utzon's Bagsvaerd Church notable for its metaphoric sunrise over the sea. By their need to relate to the past and to place, museums have also often been especially sensitive to the meaning of their location and heightening the visitor's experience. This sensation is one that can be shared, and the architect's job may be to build a large-scale container of space and people that, like Lina Bo Bardi's SESC leisure centre or Doshi's academic centre in Bangalore, suggests the experience of being in a landscape.

Building with a regard for landscape is not merely sentimental escapism, but arguably a more serious form of engagement with people than the more apparently sophisticated tasks of satisfying demands for high status 'iconic' urban buildings. Conventional building can disturb ecosystems in sensitive places, neglect to serve local populations or underestimate natural dangers. It seems appropriate, therefore, to group with some of the icons of place-sensitive architecture a few projects where design skill has been applied to the needs of landscape and the celebration of man's coexistence with it, as in Glen Murcutt's visitor centre, Shigeru Ban's replacement cathedral of cardboard tubes, and one of the works created by Rural Studio in Hale County, Alabama.

Bagsvaerd Church, near Copenhagen, 1968–76

—

Jørn Utzon (1918–2008)

—

The parish wanted to replace the church, demolished for its stone at the time of the Reformation, and selected Utzon, who had recently returned from Australia (see page 144). The concrete roof, held between two parallel walls, billows upwards to concealed clerestory windows. Whiteness pervades, apart from the wooden benches and carpets, ceramics and other decorations by the architect's daughter, Lin.

Hedmark Museum, Hamar, Norway, 1967–2005

—

Sverre Fehn (1924–2009)

—

Sverre Fehn worked in a manner similar to Scarpa's interventions in historic buildings (see page 190, and opposite) to enable visitors to see and understand the remains of a rare northerly monastery on a medieval trade route. A concrete walkway takes visitors over the excavated ground surface in a huge barn-like structure, introducing displays in side rooms along the way. Fehn completed the main building work in 1973, but continued to work on the site intermittently until 2005.

Brion Cemetery extension, San Vito d'Altivolte, Treviso, Italy, 1968–78

—

Carlo Scarpa (1906–78)

—

Monuments to the dead challenge simplistic assumptions about functionalism and draw the Modern architect into a delicate and ambiguous play of symbols. For the electronics manufacturer Giuseppe Brion, Carlo Scarpa created a small but complex sequence of concrete shapes and moving metal gates, a mixture of materials both precious and ordinary, in an austere garden-like setting.

**Maison Médicale ('La Mémé'),
University of Louvain, Brussels,
1970–72**

—

Lucien Kroll (b.1927)

—

Lucien Kroll rebelled against the
formalism of Modern architecture
on functional and political grounds
by involving building users,
especially in terms of pathways
and opportunities for social
contact. He wrote: 'Everything
communicates and opens, each
element sees and can understand
and meet the other.' The residence
for medical students followed
their own choices about room
arrangements, and the building
deliberately looks unfinished.

**SESC Pompéia Leisure Centre,
São Paulo, Brazil, 1977–86**

—

Lina Bo Bardi (1914–92)

—

Late in her career, Italian-born
Bo Bardi converted an oil drum
factory to house sports, cultural
and educational activities. The
architect Marcelo Ferraz writes,
'[her] approach was a genuine
revolution in the modus operandi
of contemporary architectural
practice. We had an office inside
the building itself; the project and
the programme were formulated
as an amalgam, joined and
inseparable … it was architecture
made real, experienced in
every detail.'

Byker Wall Estate, Newcastle-upon-Tyne, 1968–82
—
Ralph Erskine (1914–2005) and Vernon Gracie (birth date unknown)
—
Anxiety over the consequences of replacing traditional streets of housing with large blocks of anonymous flats grew in Britain in the late 1960s. As well as unappealing materials and forms, lack of engagement of future residents was seen as a problem. Byker was to change that, with an Anglo-Swedish architectural firm putting their office in a corner shop and adding colour and personal touches to the 'barrier block' at the top of the site that drops informally down to smaller sections in a landscaped setting.

National Art Schools, Cubanacán, Havana, Cuba, 1962–65

—

School of Theatre, Roberto Gottardi (b.1927); School of Plastic Arts and School of Modern Dance, Ricardo Porro (1925–2014); School of Ballet and School of Music, Vittorio Garatti (b.1927)

—

In 1961, Fidel Castro played a round of golf with Che Guevara at the previously exclusive Havana Country Club, and they decided what a fine setting the course would make for a school of the arts, open to all without payment. The project was begun in haste, using bricks for vaults rather than concrete, which was scarce. It was only partially completed when economic and political changes

caused a suspension and much of the building was reclaimed by jungle. Outside interest in the project and its place as the most representative building of the Cuban revolution grew in the 1990s, and work has been done to complete the buildings.

Kanchanjunga Apartments, Mumbai, 1970–83

—

Charles Correa (1930–2015)

—

Correa worked to achieve a modern architecture suitable for India's climate and culture. He was committed to avoiding artificial cooling where possible, and to finding appropriate building forms for different sections of the population. In the 85-metre (280-foot)-tall Kanchanjunga Apartments in his home town, interlocking levels allowed for open-air spaces within the building and on its perimeter, with a free flow of air. Correa was Mumbai's chief architect in the early 1970s and designed Navi Mumbai, a new town across the harbour, attempting to mix social classes and maintain the lively quality of street life.

214

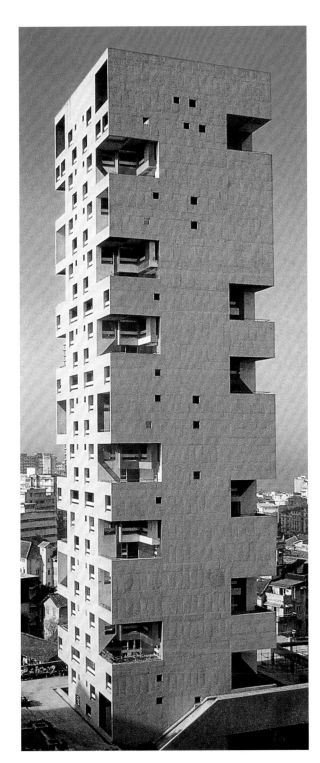

Academic Block of Indian Institute of Management, Bangalore, India, 1962–74

—

Balkrishna Vithaldas Doshi (b.1927)

—

Born in Pune, Doshi worked with Le Corbusier in Paris and returned to Ahmedabad to supervise the construction of his designs, later working closely with Louis Kahn (see page 220). In designing this building, Doshi said his aim was 'to create an atmosphere where you don't see divides and doors', using green corridors that encourage interaction. The building conserves energy by using natural ventilation and shade.

**Domus, Museum of Mankind,
La Coruña, Galicia, Spain,
1993–95**
—
Arata Isosaki (b.1931)
—
Isosaki worked with Kenzō Tange
and was part of the Metabolist
movement; he has built in Japan
and elsewhere in the world. The
Casa del Hombre is a museum
'experience' about the human
species on the north coast of Spain,
perched on a rocky promontory
with a broad sail-like roof, clad in
slate tiles, facing out to sea, with an
indented profile towards the land.
It is one of many buildings that
demonstrate that an outsider can
interpret the quality of place as
well as a locally based architect.

216

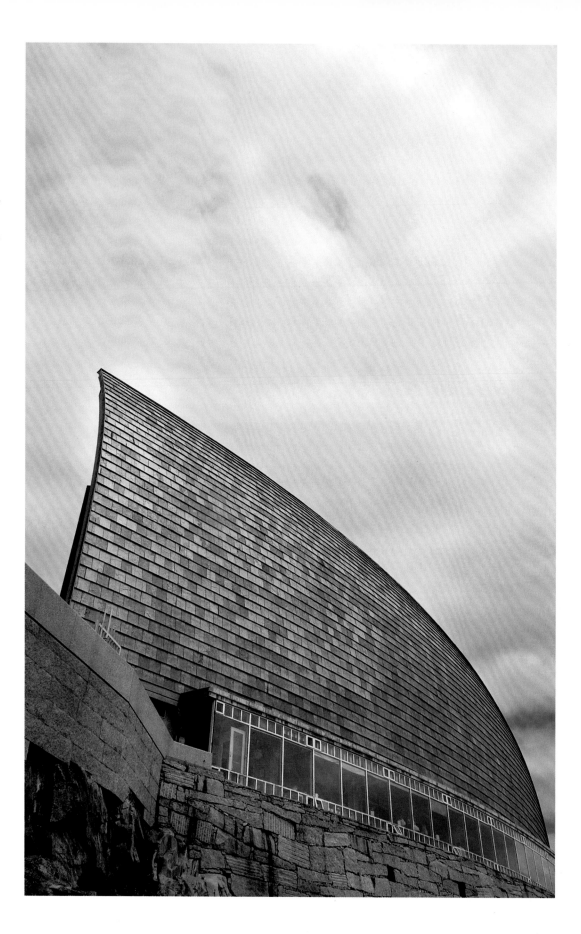

Farkasréti Cemetery Chapel, Budapest, 1975
—
Imre Makowecz (1935–2011)
—
As a protest against the uniformity of architecture in Hungary under Communism, Makowecz reverted to the National Romantic style of 1900, with an emphasis on timber construction and dramatic shapes both inside and out. He was banned from working in Budapest in 1975, and moved to the north of the country. After 1989 his work became globally known through the efforts of an English journalist, Jonathan Glancey, who described him as 'at once fierce and kind, intensely serious and very funny'.

Quinta da Malagueira, Évora, Portugal, 1973–77

—
Álvaro Siza Vieira (b.1933)

—
After the return of democracy to Portugal in 1974, Siza was commissioned to build a new housing settlement at Quinta da Malagueira, outside the Roman walls of Évora. The back-to-back two-storey courtyard houses provide a unified feeling while allowing for internal change. Siza created an aqueduct, echoing a sixteenth-century one that supplies the town, carrying water and cabling through the settlement, allowing for insertions below and shaded pathways.

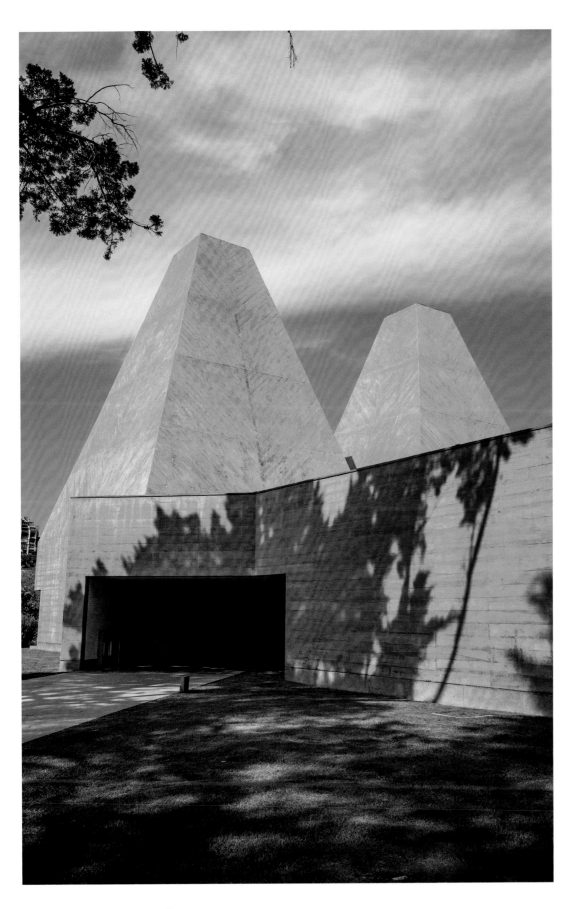

Casa das Histórias Paula Rego, Cascais, Portugal, 2008–09
—
Eduardo Souto da Moura (b.1952)
—

Born and trained in Porto, Souto de Moura worked with Alvaro Siza Vieira before establishing his own practice. The artist Paula Rego was born in Portugal in 1935 but moved to England to study at the Slade School, and is known for her disturbing narrative pictures, reflecting the brutality of the Salazar regime in Portugal. The museum of her work is described as a 'house of stories', designed to reflect local building traditions, with striking red pyramid roofs.

Church of St John the Baptist, Mogno, ValleMaggia, Ticino, Switzerland, 1994–96

—

Mario Botta (b.1943)

—

Born in Italian-speaking Switzerland, where he has built most of his work, Botta was trained in Milan and Venice. He has favoured cylindrical shapes, often making them decorative with banded masonry in contrasting tones. These have created a 'Ticino School' without necessarily deriving from local tradition. The church at Mogno replaced one that was lost when an avalanche destroyed it and a small group of houses, abandoned at the time, in 1986. The elliptical cylinder is lit from its oblique lid, and stands against a mountain background.

Indian Institute of Management, Vastrapur, Ahmedabad, Gujurat, India, 1962–74

—

Louis Kahn (1901–74)

—

Kahn was working on the new government buildings in Dacca when he was approached by Balkrishna Doshi to design the IIM at Ahmedabad, on which they worked together. As with Doshi's building for the same institution in Bangalore (see page 215), the circulation spaces were seen as crucial to the learning function of the building. While the business school curriculum was modern, the architecture was suggestive of the ruins of a distant past, with circular openings in the massive brick walls, emphasized by concrete strainer beams.

Thermal Baths, Vals, Graubunden, Switzerland, 1993–96

—

Peter Zumthor (b.1943)

—

After studying in New York, Zumthor became a historic buildings architect, carrying from this experience and his own background in carpentry a rare sense of the potential of simple materials. He is known for his thoughtful, unflashy approach to light, space and texture, based on personal experience. Evocative images of the layered slate walls inside the natural hot baths conveyed late twentieth-century architecture's yearning for the sensual and timeless.

21_21 Design Sight, 9-7-6 Akasaka, Minato-ku, Tokyo, 2007

—

Tadao Ando (b.1941)

—

Created jointly by the fashion designer Issey Miyake and Tadao Ando, the 21_21 is a design museum and exhibition space, most of which is below ground level, under the two triangular steel planes of the roof, which are meant to suggest the small pleats that Miyake has made one of his signatures. Ando has consciously sought to incorporate aspects of traditional Japanese architecture in his use of modern materials – above all, finely crafted concrete – and the way his buildings relate to landscape.

Kempsey Museum and Visitor Information Centre, New South Wales, Australia, 1976–88

—

Glen Murcutt (b.1936)

—

Climate and history have made the Australian relationship to the earth a sensitive one, and Murcutt was a pioneer in working for a sustainable form of architecture that would touch the earth lightly. He works as a one-man practitioner, but has achieved worldwide fame for the ingenuity and integrity of his designs. The Kempsey building orients visitors to the Macleay Valley, midway between Sydney and Brisbane. The simple shed forms, using timber frame and metal sheeting, reproduce the typical materials and shapes of European settlers in Australia.

Downland Gridshell, Weald and Downland Open Air Museum, Singleton, West Sussex, 2002

—

Edward Cullinan (b.1931) and Partners with BuroHappold engineers (founded 1976)

—

The Weald and Downland Museum researches and exhibits vernacular buildings, mostly with timber frames. Storage, workshop and display space were needed, and Cullinan's Gridshell reinvented the timber frame technique with a diagonal grid of green oak, built flat and pulled into shape by weights over formwork. The cedar cladding was similarly shaped to fit the giant peanut shape. The result was a balance between old and new, with only 3 per cent of the embodied energy of an equivalent steel and concrete structure.

Red Location Museum, New Brighton, Port Elizabeth, South Africa, 2005

—

Noero Wolff Architects (Jo Noero, b.1949, and Heinrich Wolff, b.1970)

—

Red Location is a poor black suburb in the Cape Town conurbation, originally a Boer War concentration camp named after its rusting iron roofs. The museum commemorates the anti-Apartheid movement connected with the area and uses the everyday local materials and forms – concrete blocks and corrugated iron, under an industrial-style sawtooth roof. It aims to involve individual memories in understanding a painful past and present, using the 'memory box', based on the boxes storing precious items left behind by migrant workers. Many local people, a large percentage of whom lived in poverty, staged protests against the amount of money spent on the museum. These protests culminated in the museum's closure in 2014.

Scottish Parliament building, Edinburgh, 1999–2004

—

Enric Miralles (1955–2000) and Benedetta Tagliabue (b.1963)

—

A parliament building for a country seeking to assert its identity in contrast to a dominant neighbour carried a heavy burden and involved a number of explicit references to aspects of Scottish landscape and culture to create decorative complexity that has not always found favour, since its symbolism stands close to kitsch. The Catalan architect had a national background with much in common with Scotland, in the way that Charles Rennie Mackintosh and Antoni Gaudí may be seen as cognate contemporaries.

226

Katrina Cottage, 2005

—

Marianne Cusato (b.1974)

Cusato took part in an emergency design exercise after Hurricane Katrina in 2005, organized by Andrés Duany, one of the inventors of New Urbanism. The federal government was sending metal trailers as relief housing, and Duany suggested that Cusato should design a traditional timber cabin that would be cheap, appropriate to the climate, and the nucleus for expansion on any devastated plot of land. Mississippi has built 2,800 Katrina Cottages, and the design is popular as a home annexe.

$20K House, Alabama, 2009

—

Rural Studio (founder Samuel Mockbee, 1944–2001)

A native of Mississippi, Mockbee was affected by the Civil Rights Movement and committed his design and teaching career to helping poor communities. In 1992 he founded Rural Studio with D. K. Ruth in Alabama, where he was teaching, 'to enable each student to step across the threshold of misconceived opinions and to design/build with a "moral sense" of service to a community'. Donated and recycled materials, including hay bales, carpets and car tyres, were often used in construction.

Christchurch Transitional
Cathedral, New Zealand, 2013
—
Shigeru Ban (b.1957)
—
Ban's use of cardboard tubes
is an intellectual gesture as well
as a humanitarian and ecological
one. Since these are often discarded
after use, they are cheaply available
to build structures after natural
disasters, and Ban has specialized
in this work in Turkey and Rwanda.
His Japanese Pavilion for the
Hannover Expo 2000 was also
made from cardboard. The 2011
Christchurch earthquake damaged
the Victorian cathedral, and this
temporary cardboard replacement
was the first major post-earthquake
building in the city.

10
—
High Tech
and
Low Tech
—
1975—
2014

Willis Faber Dumas Offices, Ipswich, Suffolk, England, 1971–75

—

Foster + Partners (Norman Foster, b.1935), perspective by Helmut Jacoby (1926–2005), 1972

—

Helmut Jacoby's meticulous pen-and-ink perspectives were popular with American architects in the 1950s. He had retired when Norman Foster sought him out to draw his most famous early building, dripping with vegetation that never actually found a place inside this atrium, suggestive of a luxury hotel or airport, with its gliding escalators replacing the standard lift and stairs.

The architectural phenomenon of High Tech was acclaimed in the 1970s and 1980s as the true heir of an otherwise discredited Modernism. This was a movement with origins in the interwar period, in such buildings as the Maison de Verre (known to Richard Rogers when living in Paris to build the Centre Pompidou) and the Maison du Peuple at Clichy, whose technical wizard, Jean Prouvé, influenced the selection of the Centre Pompidou design and advised the architects, Piano and Rogers, during its gestation. Later, it was in scientifically advanced and free-thinking California that the idea of big, undifferentiated spaces held on light steel space frames, with roof voids carrying pipework for services, offered one of the fundamental principles of High Tech – that of bringing previously hidden aspects of buildings into view and letting them become a form of decoration. The precision of metal structure and cladding, clipped or screwed together with panes of glass popped like car windscreens into neoprene housings, was a relief from the messiness of poured concrete or laborious bricklaying, and offered opportunities for bright colours to go with the Pop Art mood of the time.

High Tech architects such as Norman Foster were radical thinkers in terms of how the free open spaces of their interiors would make work both more pleasurable and more democratic than in the subdivided office buildings of the time, while the style's display of engineering struts and cables, evoking early aviation, still makes it a popular choice for airport terminals.

At one end of the spectrum, High Tech became a dazzling decorative style beneath the cloak of Modernism, as seen in Eva Jiřičná's range of fashion and jewellery shops. At the other end is its counterpart, which we can describe as low tech, or green tech. As parts of the architectural profession have begun to confront the need to save energy and resources, a section of the High Tech movement has joined the wider movement for green architecture. Large firms that have grown from small beginnings in the London of the 1970s, such as those established by Nicholas Grimshaw and Michael Hopkins, have made this a leading motif of their practices, while one of Britain's most evangelical green architects, Bill Dunster, began his career with Hopkins before branching off to create an exemplary housing project at BedZED. He and Ken Yeang are both among the advocates of the energy-conscious high-rise, harnessing the potential of wind above the streets and the action of rising heat within the building. Even more dramatically, Stefano Boeri's Bosco Verticale shows how refreshing an outbreak of overhead greenery can be for the streets of a city.

Green architecture has many other strategies, however. There is the repurposing of existing buildings, such as the modest architectural offices of Sjölander da Cruz, or the recycling of shipping containers in a number of structures around the world. Herzog & de Meuron's New North Zealand hospital in rural Denmark is a low-rise continuous clover-shaped structure in a lush landscape setting in which nature will be a resource not only for the building but for the well-being of the patients.

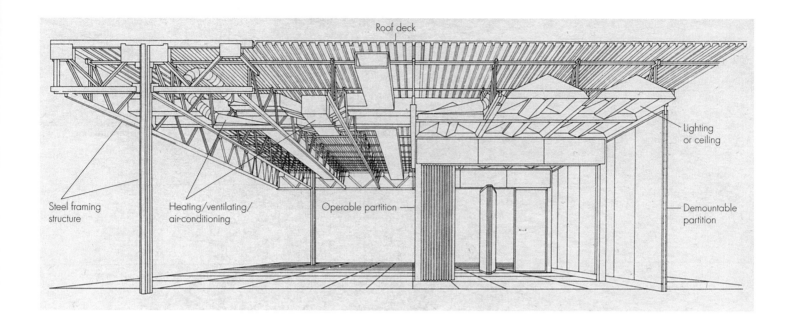

Roof deck

Steel framing structure

Heating/ventilating/ air-conditioning

Operable partition

Lighting or ceiling

Demountable partition

232 **California School System Design, 1964**

—

Ezra Ehrenkrantz (1932–2001)

—

The drawing of this constructional system, sharing some characteristics with the 1940s Hertfordshire schools in England (see page 170), added a roof zone within the height of the lightweight girders, deep enough to contain all the building services (wiring, ducting, lighting) in a way that could show them off as features while also making them easily accessible for repair or replacement. This invention was one of the bases for the High Tech designs of Foster, Rogers and others.

Eames House, 203 North Chautauqua Boulevard, Pacific Palisades, California, 1949

—

Charles Eames (1907–78) and Ray Eames (1912–88)

—

Having planned a more conventional modern house with Eero Saarinen in 1945, to be built of industrial components, the Eames preferred a simpler scheme using the same parts, which became the California Case Study House No.8 (see also page 175). Coloured panels in a black steel frame characterize the exterior, while the interior opened up the light-filled space.

Willis Faber Dumas Offices, Ipswich, Suffolk, England, 1971–75
—
Foster + Partners (Norman Foster, b.1935)
—
Early in their careers, Norman Foster and Richard Rogers abandoned conventional 'wet' construction and designed buildings that would clip together. This required technical innovation, driven by aesthetic goals. Willis Faber Dumas followed the shape of the site for the sake of economy, using glass that was reflective by day but transparent at night. It restored glamour to the idea of commercial building.

233

Centre Pompidou, place de Beaubourg, Paris, 1971–77

—

Renzo Piano (b.1937) and Richard Rogers (b.1933), with engineer Peter Rice (1935–92) of Arup

—

A culmination of the 1960s zeal for novelty and reshaping institutions, the Centre Pompidou aimed to be all things to all people – as much an experience as a museum. Won in competition and modified pragmatically in execution – saved by Peter Rice's invention of the steel 'gerberette' to hold up the structure – the verve of the concept won over the public with its proposal that culture was fun, with the entertaining, if largely unnecessary, device of putting all the services on the outside as a form of decoration.

Cummins Engine Factory, Shotts, Glasgow, 1980

—

ABK (Peter Ahrends, b.1933, Richard Burton, b.1933, and Paul Koralek, b.1933)

—

Cummins Diesel, makers of motors, are a US firm with a strong record of architectural patronage. They commissioned Kevin Roche, Eero Saarinen's successor, to build their first UK plant at Darlington in 1965, and followed with ABK's design to convert a textile factory, with views out to the landscape for the workers. Using concrete, metal-framed glazing and coloured steel, the building (abandoned in 1996 but protected and reused), is conceptually parallel to High Tech.

**Gare de Saint-Exupéry
(formerly Gare de Satolas),
Lyon, 1989–94**

—

Santiago Calatrava (b.1951)

—

Linking airport and TGV, this
station displays the Spanish
architect-engineer's skill in
designing memorable structures
that often resemble enormous
animal skeletons. Calatrava's
bridges around the world in the
1990s (including examples in
Dublin and Venice) struck an
emotional chord with the public.

236

Terminal One, Kansai International Airport, Osaka, 1991–94

—

Renzo Piano Building Workshop (Renzo Piano, b.1937) and Noriaki Okabe (b.1947), with engineers Peter Rice (1935–92) and Tom Barker (b.1966) of Arup

—

A controversial project on an artificial island in the sea, this terminal, which was the longest in the world at the time, pioneered an aerofoil roof devised by Peter Rice to aid natural ventilation, avoiding the need for ducting and thus revealing the curved shape. The runways are fully visible from the booking hall and the departure areas.

Commerzbank Tower, Frankfurt, 1991–97

—

Foster + Partners (Norman Foster, b.1935)

—

At the time of planning, the Green Party was influential in the city government, and encouraged a new approach to building an office tower. There is a double skin of glass, allowing for the circulation of air between them, and there are three 'sky gardens' with trees and other plants, which make the building more pleasant to be in and allow natural light to penetrate deeper into the floors. The plan form is triangular, with lifts and stairs in the corners.

**Institut du Monde Arabe,
rue des Fossés-Saint-Bernard,
Paris, 1981–87**

—

**Architecture-Studio (founded
1973), with Jean Nouvel (b.1945)**

—

The institute was founded in
1981 to disseminate information
about the culture of the Arab
world. Its headquarters was won
in competition by Nouvel as his
first major project. The memorable
device on the large south-facing
wall was to create a sunscreen
with perforated metal plates,
which are controlled to open and
close in response to light levels.
This provides an Arab feel to the
building without being a literal
historical copy.

Schlumberger Gould Research Centre (Phase 1), Cambridge, England, 1992

—

Hopkins Architects (Michael Hopkins, b.1935, and Patricia Hopkins, b.1942)

—

Hopkins was the project architect for Foster for Willis Faber Dumas (see page 230), and has developed the principles of High Tech in some unexpected directions. The Schlumberger Centre, with its stretched roof of Teflon-coated glass fibre, encloses separate structures within, allowing generous circulation to encourage interaction among staff, and sufficient height for the building's function of testing drilling equipment. Illuminated at night, it is an attractive addition to the western fringe of Cambridge.

Boodles House (formerly Boodle and Dunthorne), Lord Street, Liverpool, 2004

—

Eva Jiřičná (b.1939)

—

Moving from Prague to London as a young architect, Eva Jiřičná became famous for a series of shop interiors for the fashion designer Joseph Ettedgui in London in the 1980s that contributed to making High Tech a style associated with luxury and consumerism. The Liverpool-based jewellers, Boodle and Dunthorne, founded in 1798, were developing branches in several cities and used her designs to project a modern image, including the acrobatic staircase in their Liverpool main branch.

**Mesiniaga Tower, Subang Jaya,
Selangor, Malaysia, 1989–92**
—
Ken Yeang (b.1948)
—

Born in Malaysia but educated
mainly in England, Ken Yeang
was a pioneer in studying how to
mitigate the ecological impact of
buildings, writing *Designing with
Nature* in 1995. By maximizing
natural effects of shading and
ventilation, mechanical air-
conditioning, a major contributor
to greenhouse gases, is avoidable.
The Mesiniaga Tower, a 'bioclimatic
skyscraper', pioneered sky terraces
as used by Foster in Frankfurt,
and optimizes solar orientation,
placing the lift core to shield the
office floors, facilitating up draught
and including an evaporative
cooling pool on the roof.

BedZED, London Road, Hackbridge, Surrey, England, 2000–02

—

Bill Dunster Architects / ZEDfactory (Bill Dunster, b.1960)

—

This is a demonstration project by an architect committed to helping people reduce their ecological footprint in a holistic way, coupling low energy use in the home to the reduction of carbon emissions in travel and food. The terraces have a complex cross section to include 82 homes, variously configured, all facing the sun, with individual outdoor spaces, plus live–work spaces on the shaded side. Heat-exchanging ventilation cowls and photovoltaic panels mean that residents pay little or nothing for winter heating. They also have access to shared electric cars.

The Urban House, 2014

—

Mujirushi Ryohin (founded 1979)

—

The international design brand Muji (short for Mujirushi Ryohin, or 'no brand goods') offered its first house in 2000, aimed at the Japanese market, with its culture of replacing old houses for each new owner. Without changing this pattern, the Muji house helps by providing a cheaper prefabricated solution. The Urban House, shown here, maximizes the footprint of under 400 square feet (37 square metres) by omitting partitions and using split levels. The exterior is well insultated, reducing heating costs.

Bosco Verticale, Via Gaetano di Castillia and Via Federico Confalonieri, Porta Nuova, Milan, 2009–14

—

Stefano Boeri (b.1956), with Gianandrea Barreca (b.1969) and Giovanni La Varra (b.1967)

—

Milan has a tradition of trees growing on roof terraces. The benefits of trees in cities are well recognized, supporting biodiversity and air quality, mitigating 'urban heat island effect' and improving mental well-being. Bosco Verticale extends this to all levels of the high rise in order to add some 730 trees plus shrubs and other plants in the two residential towers, the equivalent of 1 hectare (2.5 acres) of woodland.

Via Verde, 700–704 Brook Ave at East 156th Street, Bronx, New York, 2006–12

—

Dattner Architects (founder Richard Dattner, b.1937) and Grimshaw Architects (founder Sir Nicholas Grimshaw, b.1939)

—

Winner of a design competition for affordable, low-energy dense urban housing, addressing health issues among urban residents, Via Verde is on a narrow triangular plot in South Bronx, an area noted for poverty and urban decay. The building climbs from town houses at the lower end to 20 storeys of apartments with roof gardens spiralling upwards, available for food growing and as community spaces, as well as providing insulation and collection of storm water. Cross ventilation reduces the need for air-conditioning.

Kroon Hall School of Forestry and Environmental Studies, Yale University, New Haven, Connecticut, 2009

—

Hopkins Architects (Michael Hopkins, b.1935, and Patricia Hopkins, b.1942), with Centerbrook Architects (founded 1973)

—

Kroon Hall combines two specialisms of Hopkins Architects: contextual design in sensitive locations, and the integration of energy-saving systems, pioneered when Bill Dunster was in the office in the 1990s. The stone-clad walls match the adjacent Ivy League Gothic buildings, while the humpback roof answers Eero Saarinen's hockey stadium. The building includes timber sourced from Yale's own forests; heating, cooling and renewable generation features; gardens and facilities to reduce the impact on users of this and adjacent buildings.

River Studio, Leamington Spa, England, 2013

—

Sjölander da Cruz Architects (Maria Sjölander, b.1967, and Marco da Cruz, b.1968)

—

In contrast to international prestige projects, these architects' offices show how a low-grade agricultural building can be kept (avoiding loss of embodied energy in the original structure) and 're-purposed' to create a pleasant, low-energy working space clad in cedar boards, built to Passivhaus EnerPHit standards. Older buildings in daily use are often highly inefficient in energy terms, and the task of retrofitting them is an urgent one.

New North Zealand Hospital, Hillerød, Denmark, 2014–

—

Herzog & de Meuron (Jacques Herzog, b.1950, Pierre de Meuron, b.1950, Christine Binswanger, b.1964, Ascan Mergenthaler, b.1969, and Stefan Marbach, b.1970), with Vilhelm Lauritzen Arkitekter (founder Vilhelm Lauritzen, 1894–1984)

—

Herzog and de Meuron became famous in Basel, originally preferring a restrained minimalist style, but over time becoming more expressive in their forms and materials. The hospital is surrounded by nature and contains a garden in its centre. The building's undulating linear form mimics the surrounding landscape. The horizontal building fosters an exchange between the departments of the hospital, encouraging the employees' shared goal: the healing of the ailing human being.

**Le Utthe Boutique, La Plata,
Argentina, 2015**

—

BBC Arquitectos (dates unkown)

—

Steel shipping containers are
a global utility product that
wears out in original use but
remains serviceable for purposes
of habitation and storage. This
fashion shop is close to the port
and wanted an industrial look
because they manufacture all their
stock themselves. The boxes are
suspended to reflect their original
purpose, and shoppers can enter
them to browse displays and use
changing rooms.

11
—
Icons, Superstars and Global Brands

—

1980—
2014

Daniel Libeskind's publication *Chamber Works* was sponsored by the Architectural Association in London where, under the leadership of Alvin Boyarsky, Rem Koolhaas and Zaha Hadid were among students who revelled in the freedom to forget the requirements of use, construction or gravity in favour of brilliant and often obscure drawings that suggested immense difficulty and skill. Libeskind describes the drawings as 'drifting in a no-man's land between reality and dreams, the world of the unknown'.

For most of the past 100 years, just a handful of architects were known by name to the general public at any time, in contrast to the names of sports or music stars. One consequence of the crisis of Modernism at the end of the 1960s was to suggest to certain individuals that more attention-grabbing designs, coupled with a cult of personality that was alien to many of the socially motivated designers of the middle years of the century, might be good for their profession and for themselves. So it has proved to be. The Sydney Opera House propelled its designers to fame for good or ill in the 1950s, but the 1980s and 1990s brought a flood of buildings around the world by architects who understood the attraction of unusual shapes. Their intellectually austere wing was represented by Peter Eisenman, while on a more popular level, François Mitterrand's 'Grands Projets' in Paris shamed the parsimony of other cities.

The word 'icon' came in during the 1990s, most often applied to cultural landmarks after the Sydney model. 'Bilbao' became no longer just a city in the Basque region of Spain, but shorthand for an icon parachuted into a struggling post-industrial city with the hope of generating tourist income. Frank Gehry's original was undoubtedly successful for business, both for the city and for himself, and has generated many imitators.

From the beginning of the century, most Modern architecture was in league with the camera to achieve its mission of persuasion. The superstar architects relished the temptation to create simple images, which have picked up nicknames such as the 'Bird's Nest' stadium for the Beijing Olympics, and played a part in the recent outbreak of novelty skyscrapers in London. It was not photography that had changed, but the quantity of images now easily available and the speed with which they could be circulated that began to change with the onset of the internet in the 1990s, the period when a distinctive 'iconic' kind of architecture developed.

There is no official definition for an icon building, and many that appear in other sections of this book might qualify as easily as those included in this chapter, but the names of certain architects are closely linked to the phenomenon. In many ways, the icon cult was a way of bringing back into architecture more imagination and licence to compose with artistic freedom, as illustrated by Will Alsop, whose designs begin as paintings, or Gehry, transforming crumpled paper into computer-coded templates for construction. For the Jewish Museum in Berlin, the theme required a sensitive and relevant iconography, developed by Daniel Libeskind with a great formal complexity that can still be understood by visitors as an experience. Rem Koolhaas, Zaha Hadid and Libeskind belong to a generation that studied in London at an extraordinary time and have left their mark across the world. Their work can now be supported by 'parametric design' using computer algorithms to generate complex curved surfaces, seen by its advocates as heralding a new era of design.

Wexner Center for the Arts, Ohio State University, 1983–88

Peter Eisenman (b.1932)

—

During the 1970s, Eisenman was involved in developing architecture and its discourse to the furthest remove from the everyday or pragmatic by recycling some of the motifs of early Modernism to become the components of complex abstract formal games that acquired the name Deconstructivism. The overlaid grids at different angles that are found in the Wexner Center, Eisenman's first major building, are typical of his belief that 'architecture does not answer questions, it asks questions. It does not solve problems, it creates problems.'

Guggenheim Museum, Bilbao, 1981–97

Frank Gehry (b.1929)

—

Unforgettably eye-catching and highly effective in its mission to boost cultural tourism, the Bilbao Guggenheim is the archetypal 'icon' building. Taking curvaceous hints from Frank Lloyd Wright's New York original, it discards Cartesian grid thinking in favour of intuitive form-making that is, for all its apparent arbitrariness, closely related to the physical context of river, hills and city, and reflects ambient light from its titanium panels. Fabrication was enabled by computer programs intended for aircraft.

The Jewish Museum, Berlin, 1989–2001
—
Daniel Libeskind (b.1946)
—
Libeskind has said that 'if there is no story then [a building] is just a hunk of metal, glass, and concrete. ... Every building, every city should have a story – a story about lives, about people. Otherwise a building is an object, an abstraction.' The experience of the often uncomfortable and irrational spaces within the fragmented silver-skinned Berlin building constitutes the first part of the visitor's experience, later moving to the upper levels to view more conventional museum objects. The insistence on narrative reverts to nineteenth-century notions of the didactic purpose of a public building.

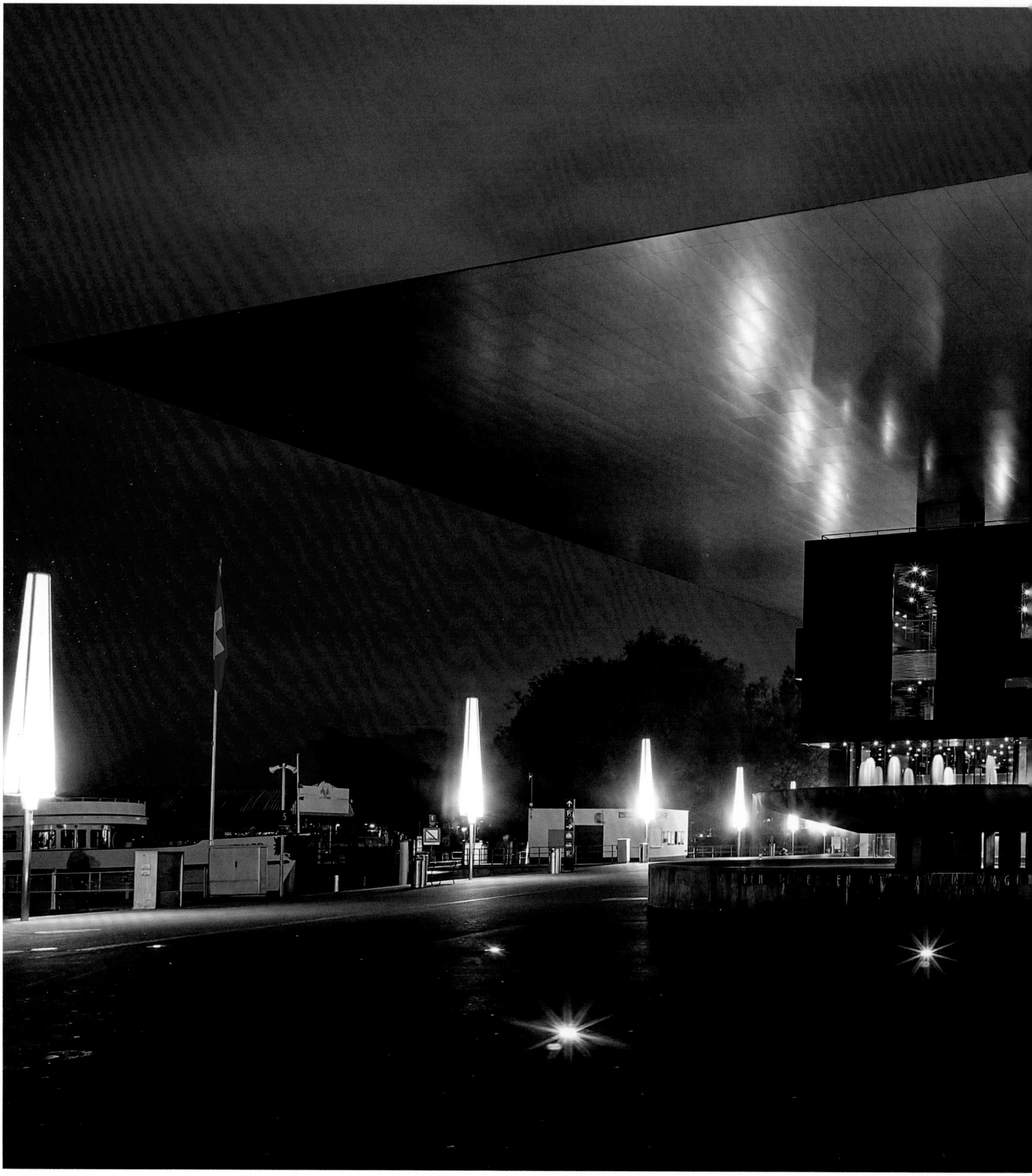

Cultural and Congress Centre, Europlatz, Lucerne, Switzerland, 1993–2000
—
Ateliers Jean Nouvel (b.1945)
—
The oversailing roof of this waterside concert hall complex reflects light from its aluminium underside, framing the distant views and binding together the different parts of the complex, which also includes a conference centre and a museum of contemporary art. Beneath this canopy, different colours are used for the elements of the structure.

Sendai Mediatheque, Japan, 1995–2000

—

Toyo Ito (b.1941)

—

Ito is fascinated by the potential of dense cities and urban life. The typology of the mediatheque extends the traditional public library to become a meeting place and social centre. At Sendai, Ito opened the building to full view, making each of the 12 steel lattice columns to different patterns, swaying, swelling and shrinking as they pass through the floors. The facades are fully glazed, giving the building maximum transparency at night, a symbolic as well as practical requirement of the brief.

Kunsthaus Graz, Austria, 2003

—

Peter Cook (b.1936) and Colin Fournier (b.1944)

—

The Archigram group, of which Cook was a founder in 1963, was famous for having virtually no buildings to its name. However, Cook's whimsical and provocative ideas are now academic orthodoxy. After many years of teaching, Cook was able to realize the Kunsthaus, a building with many of the functions of a mediatheque. The zoomorphic nozzles on the roof are skylights, and the blue acrylic cladding can be used for the display of digital works of art.

Casa da Música, Porto, 1999–2005
—
Rem Koolhaas (b.1944) and OMA (Office of Metropolitan Architecture) (founded 1975), with Arup (originally founded 1946)
—
Koolhaas and one of his teachers, Elia Zenghelis, a co-founder of OMA in 1975, were involved in 'paper architecture' until they began building with the Netherlands Dance Centre in 1987. Reliably shocking, Koolhaas embraces the brashness of contemporary urban life. The Casa da Música is an irregular white volume externally, housing three orchestras, while internally Koolhaas's frequent collaborator, Petra Blaisse, has contributed patterned curtains and a gigantic enlargement of wood grain for the main concert hall walls, carried out in gold leaf.

**Mercedes Benz Museum,
Stuttgart, 2001–06**
—
**UNStudio (co-founders Ben van
Berkel, b.1957, and Caroline Bos,
b.1959)**
—
The practice, founded in 1988,
contributed to the revival of Dutch
architecture in the 1990s, when
a new generation confronted the
grid-obsessed national culture
with complex geometrical shapes.
The Mercedes Benz Museum
stands at the gates of the company
factory, and its shapes evoke
the form of an off-centre Wankel
engine. Two routes through the
spaces form a descending double
helix, corresponding to two
interpretations of the story that
may be explored separately
or interchangeably.

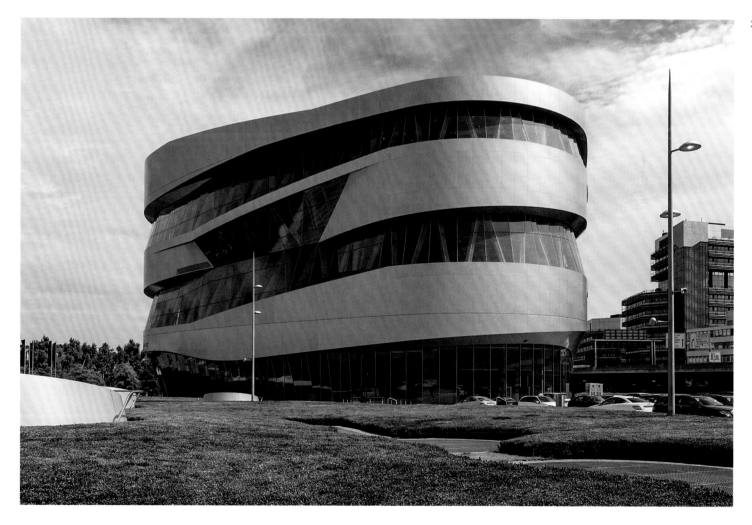

MAXXI (National Museum of XXI Century Arts), Via Guido Reni, Rome, 1998–2009

—

Zaha Hadid (1950–2016)

—

Before establishing her own practice in London, the Iraqi-born Hadid worked with OMA. Based on geometry, her designs were inspired by those of revolutionary Russia in their anticlassical forms, and she developed a fascination with flowing spaces, for which museums are an ideal typology. Hadid called MAXXI 'not an object container but rather a campus for art'. As at Bilbao (see page 252), there is a conflict between the spectacular nature of the building and the way that it limits what can successfully be shown in it.

260

Brandhorst Museum, Munich, 2005–09

—

Sauerbruch Hutton (Matthias Sauerbruch, b.1955, and Louisa Hutton, b.1957)

—

In contrast to MAXXI, which opened before it had a collection, the Brandhorst Museum was built to house a private collection given to the German state of Bavaria. The blank rectilinear walls are enlivened by a novel treatment of three-dimensional terracotta rods, their colours subtly mixed after much trial and error, to create a gentle shimmering effect. Colour is a recurrent theme in the work of this Anglo-German practice, as it has been for many architects looking to escape the conformist good taste of Modernism. Sometimes the results are brash or banal, but the Brandhorst shows the potential of a more considered approach.

Great Relic Museum, Fangshan Tangshan National Geopark Museum, Nanjing, China, 2014

—

Studio Odile Decq (b.1955)

—

This museum charts the rise of the species *Homo erectus*, displaying finds from this important archaeological site. It takes its form from the hills beyond and offers a continuous experience, with ramps rather than abrupt level changes, such as many recent museums have favoured, no doubt with accessibility in mind as much as curatorial needs.

Hôtel du Département des Bouches-du-Rhône (Le Grand Bleu), Marseilles, 1991–94

—

Alsop & Störmer (Will Alsop, b.1947, and Jan Störmer, b.1942)

—

With its extrusion-like cross section, its strong use of colour and its angled supports, Le Grand Bleu, won in competition against 156 entries, established Will Alsop's reputation, previously based on small-scale projects. It was a portent of the increasing international spread of British-based practices. To the potentially mundane housing of local bureaucracy, Alsop and his German partner of the time, Jan Störmer, brought a quality of irrationality and panache that characterized Alsop's mentor, the English visionary and controversialist Cedric Price.

Tour Crédit Lyonnais (now Tour de Lille), Euralille Business Quarter, Lille, 1991–95

—

Christian de Portzamparc (b.1944)

—

The first French winner of the Pritzker Prize for Architecture (a certification of 'iconic' status), de Portzamparc represents the post-1968 generation in France who were beneficiaries of Mitterrand's 'Grand Projets' and the transformation of brownfield sites in Paris, such as the abattoirs at La Villette, where de Portzamparc built his Cité de la Musique. The form at Euralille was derived from various constraints of the site, bridging over railway tracks, and orienting the office accommodation towards the city of Lille.

Yokohama Ferry Terminal, Japan, 1995–2002

Foreign Office Architects (Farshid Moussavi, b.1965, and Alejandro Zaera-Polo, b.1963)
—

FOA was a husband-and-wife team operating from 1993 to 2011. Winning the competition at Yokohama established their reputation, achieving one of the most acclaimed examples of spatially complex, folded architecture to date – one that had been foreshadowed in a number of writings but, before the advent of computer-aided design and construction, would have been much harder and more costly to achieve. Ramped level changes between parking, administration and the upper level viewing deck were a natural solution to the need for people to move smoothly, and the design turns them into a playful experience.

Chapel of St Ignatius, Seattle University, 1994–97
—
Steven Holl (b.1947)
—

The Jesuit chapel at Seattle established Holl's concern with light as an architectural element, influenced by the inward, reflective philosophy of phenomenology. The unseen light sources, passing at times through coloured glass, inevitably evoke comparison with Le Corbusier's chapel at Ronchamp (see page 128), sometimes to Holl's disadvantage, although there was a strong appetite in the 1990s for a softer ideology of architecture than those offered by High Tech or the more demonstrative kinds of Postmodernism.

**Netherlands Pavilion, Expo
2000, Hannover, 1997–2000**
—
**MVRDV (Winy Maas, b.1959,
Jacob van Rijs, b.1964, and
Nathalie de Vries, b.1965)**
—
World's fairs continue to offer
opportunities for eye-catching
architectural experiment, the
millennium year being linked
to projects imagining the future
under the headings 'Humanity
– Nature – Technique'. The
Netherlands pavilion explored
the theme 'Holland Creates
Space', demonstrating the national
tradition of modifying nature and
the potential for using layered
structures to add to the surface
available for growing plants and
trees. Most spectacular was the
forest area with 35 oak trees.

Borneo-Sporenburg Housing, Amsterdam, 1993–96
—
West 8 (Adriaan Geuze, b.1960, and Paul van Beek, birth date unknown)
—
Although the landscape architecture practice West 8 has argued against the orthodoxy of high urban density and in favour of sparsely populating the countryside, the Borneo-Sporenburg housing masterplan in former docklands reinvents the Dutch typology of the vertical 'canal house', allowing for individual variation within overall constraints, and favouring the use of roof terraces, at a density of 100 units per hectare.

**La Liberté Housing and
Office Building, Groningen,
The Netherlands, 2009–11**
—
Dominique Perrault (b.1953)
—
Famous for his use of tower
bookstacks in the new National
Library in Paris, Perrault has
developed a new form of mixed-use
tower at Groningen, commissioned
by the city in order to counter the
spread of suburbia, with office
accommodation in the lower part,
and social housing above, separated
by an open zone. Like many other
buildings of their time, the elevations
play pattern-making games with
shape, colour, light and shade.

New Islington, Islington Square, Manchester, 2006
—

FAT (Fashion Architecture Taste) – Sean Griffiths (b.1966), Charles Holland (b.1969) and Sam Jacob (b.1970)
—

In 1995, the year that FAT was founded, Postmodernism was seen by most architects and critics as an unmentionable aberration of the recent past. FAT disagreed, and started using their own versions of cartoonish facade design to enliven their projects and successfully catch media attention. For the New Islington housing development, residents were consulted about their lifestyles and requirements, which were reflected in the house plans. The elevations are yet one more reinvention of the traditional and popular English urban terrace.

Mainz Market House, Germany, 2003–08
—
Massimiliano Fuksas (b.1944) and Doriana Fuksas (birth date unknown)
—

In the historic (or pseudo-historic) city centre of Mainz, the Market House mixes offices, retail and residential. White columns pass through biomorphic openings in the floor plates of the atrium, partially exposed to the weather outside. The white external skin of 5-cm (2-inch)-wide ceramic bars opens in places to reveal roof terraces. Fuksas has commented, 'I'm not afraid of context, but I don't think you can build in the center of a city without paying attention to what is already there.'

270

One World Trade Center, New York, 2006–14

—

David Childs (b.1941) of Skidmore Owings & Merrill, from a competition design by Daniel Libeskind (b.1946)

—

The destruction of Minoru Yamasaki's World Trade Center towers in 2001 did not deter the development of ever-higher prestige skyscrapers around the world. The replacement project was inevitably fraught with symbolic expectations ill-adapted to a commercially driven project, with the result that most of the features of the original Libeskind design were abandoned in reworkings by the developer's favourite architect.

272

The Leadenhall Building (The Cheesegrater), 122 Leadenhall Street, London, 2004–13

—

Rogers Stirk Harbour (project architect Graham Stirk, b.1957)

—

In 1986, Richard Rogers' Lloyd's of London opened on Leadenhall Street. Twenty years later, his practice was planning the redevelopment of the facing site, formerly a Miesian tower of the 1960s. The contrast in scale indicates how much taller buildings have been permitted to be in the insurance district in the City of London since Foster's Swiss Re (The Gherkin). These names help to win public support, amid uncertainty about the buildings' economic efficacy as well as their effect on the London skyline.

12
—
Controlled Experience
—
1989—2014

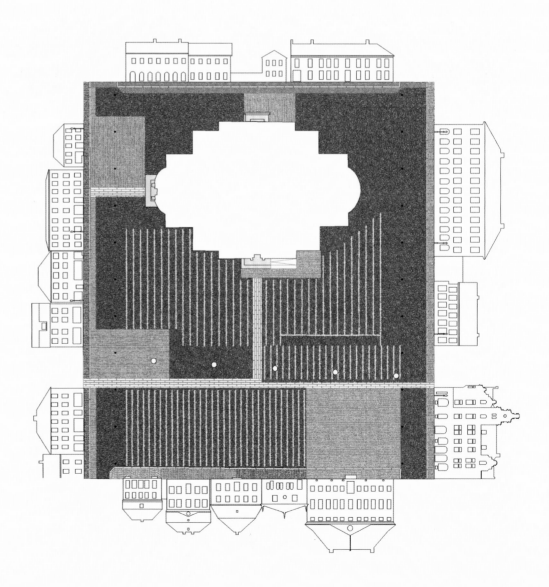

Repaving scheme for Stotorget, Kalmar, Sweden, 1999–2003
—
Caruso St John (Adam Caruso, b.1962, and Peter St John, b.1959), with artist Eva Löfdahl (b.1953)
—
Adam Caruso has written about the desirability of returning to a condition when 'before pavements, kerbs and roads, the linear ordering of the stones was a continuous field up to and around the surrounding buildings'. This drawing shows the two-dimensional effect of this recovery of a public space in a historic Swedish city, in which different paving materials subtly create their own patterns as well as referring to earlier buildings on the site.

One of the dominant strands in the discussion of architecture in the early twenty-first century has been the intersection of ethics and aesthetics, for it is in the alliance of these long-standing areas of sensitivity and expertise that architects have claimed their special position. Restraint and good taste in objects correspond to dominant moral ideas in several of the world's major belief systems, and these were fundamental to the establishment of Modernism in the years before 1914. Buildings conceived on these principles might be described as 'anti-iconic', in avoiding some of the over-obvious shapes and metaphors of the past two decades. Understatement can be more powerful than overstatement, and likely to blend better into an urban or rural setting. Buildings presenting a single material finish are popular, whether this is the white marble of Oslo's Opera House, like a ski slope by the harbour; the bent ribbon of Álvaro Siza's Jiangsu Province chemical plant; or the turned and twisted brickwork of the new Students' Union building for the LSE in London.

In the stillness of reticence, with a focus on the earth and the sky, the insistent voice of the building gives way to the framing of light and human activity. The Japanese firm SANAA's outstation for the Louvre in the ex-industrial town of Lens is an anti-Bilbao, providing little more than a floor plane and a ceiling, in this respect not unlike some buildings by Mies van der Rohe from the 1950s, but avoiding his monumentality. Robbrecht & Daem's market hall at Ghent is no more than a roof, but one that holds a civic space together. In the same way, many of the buildings shown here are place-makers – especially the two English galleries in Walsall and Wakefield, both intended as levers of regeneration and sited close to water.

The return of various forms of repetitive patterning, seen in the openings of the LSE building, the market hall and the roof of Itami Jun's Church of the Sky, is an addition to the architectural repertory present in some high-profile buildings since 2000. With its analogies to the patterns made in textile weaving, brick is again a favoured material, in line with Gottfried Semper's rediscovered theories from the nineteenth century concerning the origins of architecture in weaving rather than in the structural framework of the building.

While many images of modern buildings seem to speak of wealth and privilege, there are some that keep alive Modernism's hope that architecture could play a role in a more even distribution of the good things in life. In this context, the school in Thailand helps the rural poor in a non-patronizing way, while Michael Maltzan's housing for street sleepers on Skid Row in Los Angeles adds magic to a neglected social function. Stylistically, although not socially, Maltzan's design, with its piled-up blocks, resembles OMA's Interlace in Singapore. Rational? No, but something to remember, and even raise a smile amid the anxieties and tedium of modern life.

Centre de Soins de Jour (Daycare Centre), Bègles, Gironde, France, 1994
—
Lacaton & Vassal (Anne Lacaton, b.1955, and Jean-Philippe Vassal, b.1954)
—

In 1980, Lacaton and Vassal lived and worked in Nigeria, where they developed an affection for the beauty of simple and modest structures. The Bègles building, in a suburb of Bordeaux, is a psychiatric clinic for 18–25-year-olds. Plan and construction aimed for openness and light. The unpretentious industrial construction allowed the spaces to be more generous. The practice has since made its reputation with bold transformations of older buildings, including an art gallery and a residential tower in Paris.

Goetz Collection, Munich, 1989–92
—

Herzog & de Meuron (Jacques Herzog, b.1950, Pierre de Meuron, b.1950, Christine Binswanger, b.1964, Ascan Mergenthaler, b.1969, and Stefan Marbach, b.1970)
—

The architectural conception of the gallery corresponds to the character of the works from a single collection on display, dating from the 1960s to today. A timber structure rests on a reinforced-concrete base of the same dimension that is half buried so that only its upper glazed perimeter is visible from the outside. In the space above, as in the lower level, diffused daylight comes from matt glass that forms a band around the whole volume.

The New Art Gallery Walsall, West Midlands, England, 1997–1999
—
Caruso St John (Adam Caruso, b.1962, and Peter St John, b.1959)
—
Sculptor Jacob Epstein's personal collection belongs to Walsall, and the town took the opportunity of Millennium Commission funding to house it appropriately, with space for temporary shows, as a centrepiece of regeneration. Caruso St John made their name with the project, building a timber-lined 'house within a house', encased in a grand but muted tower, giving the town an anti-iconic landmark where a canal basin marked the loss of industry since 1945.

Abbey of Our Lady of Nový Dvůr, Bohemia, Czech Republic, 1999–2004

—

John Pawson (b.1949), with Atelier Soukup (founded 1991)

—

A commission for a new Cistercian monastery in a former Communist country sounds as far removed from the progressive ethos as can be imagined, yet Modernism has a complex ancestry whose values reflect the down-to-earth simplicity of religious life. The abbot of the new community saw pictures of a Calvin Klein shop interior by Britain's arch-minimalist, John Pawson, and realized that he would be the ideal architect to complete the courtyard of an abandoned Baroque farm.

American Folk Art Museum, West 53rd Street, New York, 2001
—
Tod Williams Billie Tsien Architects (Tod Williams, b.1943, and Billie Tsien, b.1949)
—
Williams and Tsien are known for their thoughtful, slow development of projects, often those associated with the arts, such as the new home of the Barnes Collection in Philadelphia. The American Folk Art Museum's new building next to MoMA was widely admired for its bronze-panelled facade and its displays, which were housed in a tall atrium on this narrow footprint, allowing natural light to fall on the characterful objects. Sadly, the museum was unable to pay back construction bonds after opening, and in 2011 had to sell to its powerful neighbour, which decided on demolition and redevelopment.

Filharmonia, Szczecin, Poland, 2007
—
Estudio Barozzi Veiga (Fabrizio Barozzi, b.1976, and Alberto Veiga, b.1973)
—
White is the quintessential Modernist colour, and the Filharmonia, in a town that has seen much destructive change during the 20th century, is like a ghostly vision of a wrapped Gothic castle at night, when the gap behind the milky glass and aluminium outer skin is lit up. The two auditoria inside are more strongly characterized by colour and texture, with a faceted ceiling to the Symphony Hall, developed with the acoustician Higini Arau.

**Norwegian National Opera
and Ballet, Oslo, 2000–08**
—
**Snøhetta (founding partners
Craig Edward Dykers, b.1961,
and Kjetil Traedl Thorsen, b.1958)**
—
Named after a mountain peak
in Norway, the practice, founded
in 1987, combines landscape and
architecture. The long-awaited
purpose-built home of the national
opera and ballet companies created
extra landfill in the now-redundant
harbour, looking out to sea and back
towards the city, a view that can be
enjoyed by passersby who walk up
the brilliant white slopes that form
the roof to a complex of auditoria,
rehearsal and production spaces,
with a generous front-of-house
clad in sinuous woodwork.

Church of the Sky, Jeju, South Korea, 2010

—

Itami Jun Architects (Jun Itami, 1937–2011)

—

This church stands in a developing cultural and civic centre but next to open country, to which it responds by taking the form of a simple barn, surrounded by a moat and entered at the mid-point between the worship space and the parish offices. The roofline is bowed upwards at the ends, and the patterning of its tiles has a folk-art quilt feeling, contrasting with the sobriety of the timber-framed interior.

282

The Hepworth, Wakefield, England, 2003–11

—

David Chipperfield (b.1953)

—

Built to house the fine local art collection and a major holding of sculpture and other work by Barbara Hepworth (1903–75), who was born in the South Yorkshire town, this gallery enjoys a dramatic water-girt site on the River Calder, contributing to the regeneration of a former industrial area. The grey pigmented concrete boxes reflect the shape of the upper-level galleries within, which offer framed views on to still and moving water. For many years, Chipperfield was known for building almost anywhere but in his own conservative country, but the Hepworth is one of a growing number of his UK projects.

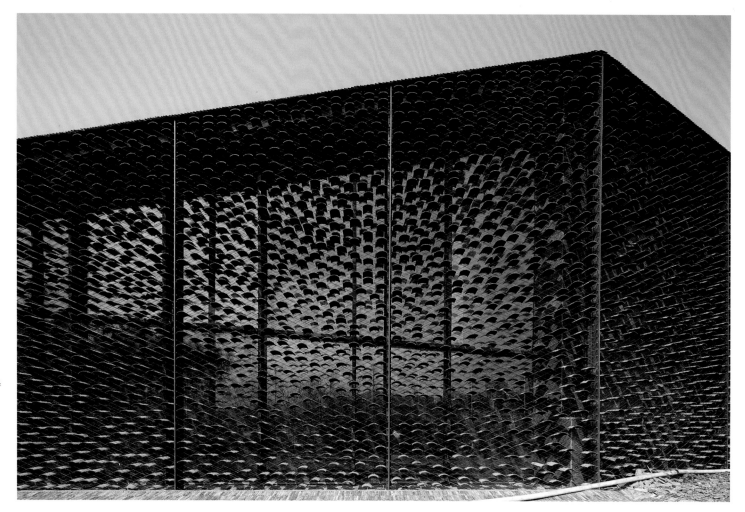

China Academy of Art Conference Centre and Museum, Hangzhou, 2014

—

Kengo Kuma (b.1954)

—

The Japanese architect Kengo Kuma aims to reinterpet historical building traditions in a non-literal way. This is seen in his addition to the Academy of Art complex at Hangzhou in Southern China, where traditional roof tiles salvaged over a number of years by his predecessor as architect on the site, Wang Shu, have been used to form a sunscreen, suspended like a flight of birds. Kuma's 2008 book, *Anti-Object*, speaks for many contemporaries with its subtitle 'the Dissolution and Disintegration of Architecture'.

Louvre-Lens, Lens, Pas-de-Calais, France, 2005–12

—

SANAA (founders Kazuyo Sejima, b.1956, and Ryue Nishizawa, b.1966), with Imrey Culbert (Celia Imrey, b.1964, and Tim Culbert, b.1960) and landscape architect Catherine Mosbach (b.1962)

—

In one of many attempts to use museum architecture to create a 'Bilbao effect', the Louvre commissioned an outstation in a depressed mining town in the Pas-de-Calais, from a Japanese practice that has been successful with its understated but visually memorable cultural buildings. The two gallery sequences are on one level, branching from the square entrance area, clad with brushed aluminium and clear glass panels with a translucent ceiling, creating an ethereal effect.

Student Centre Building, Cork Institute of Technology, Cork, Ireland, 1997–2006

—

De Blacam & Meagher (Shane de Blacam, b.1945, and John Meagher, b.1947), with Michael Kelly (b.1956)

—

Handsomely faced in lime-mortar-jointed brick, inside and out, the student centre is representative of De Blacam & Meagher's creative response to historical form and materials, poetically evocative in the manner of Louis Kahn (with whom de Blacam once worked) rather than imitative or ironic. Starting work on the campus in 1990, De Blacam & Meagher changed the existing masterplan by introducing the arc of buildings, all made of the same brick.

The Interlace, 200 Depot Road, Singapore, 2009

OMA (Ole Scheeren, b.1971, partner in charge), with RSP Architects (founded 1978)

—

Assembled like a pile of toy bricks, and reminiscent of Park Hill, Sheffield, and Habitat in Montreal (see page 172), the Interlace takes this form for the same purposes of community-building in place of the alienating effect of separate towers. The form is economical in its provision of service cores at the intersections. There is also a strong emphasis on natural growth, with ponds positioned on wind paths to cool the air by evaporation.

Helsinki University Main Library, 2012

AOA (Anttinen Oiva Arkkitehdit Oy) (Selina Anttinen, b.1977, and Vesa Oiva, b.1973)

—

The curving brick facade follows the street line and swoops up and down in relation to the lighting needs of the spaces within, with a finely detailed brick grid masking the floor heights. These elements combine to make the building both exuberant and decorous. The library brings together previously scattered resources and acts as a student centre in the middle of Helsinki. A large atrium, finished in white, rises through the height of the interior.

**Saw Swee Hock Student Centre
of London School of Economics,
London, 2013**
—
**O'Donnell & Tuomey (Sheila
O'Donnell, b.1953, and John
Tuomey, b.1954)**
—
Forming their practice in 1988
in Dublin after working for James
Stirling, the architects stimulated
discussions about regeneration,
demonstrating solutions in the
Temple Bar regeneration in the
1990s. The LSE Students' Union
is inserted in the narrow streets
that house this prestigious but
almost invisible college, so that
the dramatic brick facades were
derived in part from adjacent rights
of light, 'like they had evolved
or blown in the wind'. The free
movement of the street continues
through the interior.

Solid 11, Constantijn Huygenstraat, Amsterdam, 2011

—

Tony Fretton (b.1945)

—

'Solid' is a name given by the housing association Stadtgenoot to a residential building that, like loft apartments, provides the basic shapes and services to be fitted out by the residents or users themselves, with an expectation of mixed use as apartments, workspaces, shops and cafés. The facade is self-supporting and built for a 200-year life, its base faced in red porphyry (a nod to Adolf Loos's belief in the practicality of marble), while the upper structure is in brick. As with all of Fretton's work, subtle references underlie overtly simple forms.

Market Hall, Emilie Braunplein, Ghent, Belgium, 1996–2012

—

Robbrecht & Daem (Paul Robbrecht, b.1950, and Hilde Daem, b.1950), with Marie-José van Hee (b.1950)

—

The design team entered a competition to make a new public square in the centre of Ghent in 1996, but were disqualified because they refused to include an underground car park. This sparked protest and a change of mind, so that their executed scheme included repaving a series of interconnecting squares, and adding the Market Hall, a covered open space with a roof that looks externally like a building with two steep gables. Underneath are a café and cycle park, sending messages about the European city of the future.

Star Apartments, 240 East Sixth Street, Los Angeles, California, 2014

—

Michael Maltzan (b.1959)

—

Skid Row in Los Angeles developed in the 1930s with cheap hotels close to the freight rail yards. Attempts to 'clean up' repeatedly failed, until in 1989 the Skid Row Housing Trust began to provide better-quality single accommodation. The prefabricated design, stacked on top of an existing commercial building, is one of several projects for the Trust by LA architect Michael Maltzan, who has also worked for the local super-rich. It includes roof gardens for food production, and health facilities.

School Floating in the Sky, Sangkhlaburi, Thailand, 2013

—

Kochi University of Technology (Kikumi Watanabe, b.1971)

—

This school, close to the border with Burma, was built for the children of refugees on a very low budget and designed by students. The children were asked to visualize their future school, and an idea for a floating boat provided the inspiration for the scheme, designed by students from a Japanese university. It features three 'pods' at ground level, built using sandbags, above which rides a single room with a thatched roof, built of steel and bamboo, through which wind and sunlight can pass.

Chemical Plant Offices, Huai'an City, Jiangsu Province, China, 2009–14
—
Álvaro Siza Vieira (b.1933), with Carlos Castanheira (b.1957)
—
While Álvaro Siza is acclaimed for buildings reflecting local character in Portugal, his practice is international, challenging literal assumptions about regionality. A golf clubhouse in Taiwan led to this mainland China commission, and then to two further ones, including a Bauhaus museum in Hangzhou – an emblem perhaps of Modernism itself wrapping round time and space in a continuous loop. Looking back to Mackintosh, and Frank Lloyd Wright's desire to fertilize the moribund canon of Western architecture with influences from the East, overt distinction between the two is blurred, although it may seem as if the 'trophy' building is an unconvincing fig leaf for the vast chemical plant to which it is attached.

293

Farming Kindergarten, Dong Nai, Vietnam, 2013
—
Vo Trong Nghia (b.1976) Architects
—
Built for 500 preschool children of workers in a shoe factory next door, this kindergarten lives up to its name, with growing roofs on a gently sloping ribbon of building to ensure that at least this section of the newly urbanized population does not lose touch with its agricultural roots. The practice, founded in 2006, works in collaboration with the construction company Wind and Water House. Vo Trong Nghia has been included in an Al Jazeera English TV series on architects who are 'shunning the glamour of "starchitecture" and using design to tackle the world's urban, environmental and social crises'.

294

Further Reading

Note from the author
—
It is hard to select a small list for such a large subject. The items below include those most often consulted for selecting items for inclusion in the book, plus some of the more readily available general histories of the period.

Readers seeking further information on individual architects and buildings are recommended to search using the British Architectural Library Catalogue: http://riba.sirsidynix.net.uk/uhtbin/webcat.

Period sources
—
Behne, Adolf. *The Modern Functional Building.* (Santa Monica: Getty Research Institute, 1996.)

Behrendt, Walter Curt. *The Victory of the New Building Style.* (Santa Monica: Getty Research Institute, 2000.)

Hitchcock, Henry-Russell. *Modern Architecture: Romanticism and Reintegration.* (New York: Payson & Clarke, 1929.)

Platz, Gustav Adolf. *Die Baukunst der Nuesten Zeit,* second edition. (Berlin: Propyläen-Verlag, 1930.)

Views from the later twentieth century and after
—
Cohen, Jean-Louis. *The Future of Architecture Since 1889.* (London: Phaidon, 2012.)

Colquhoun, Alan. *Modern Architecture.* (Oxford: Oxford University Press, 2002.)

Curtis, William J. R. *Modern Architecture Since 1900,* third edition. (London: Phaidon, 1996.)

Koshalek, Richard, Elizabeth A. T. Smith and Celik Zeynep. *At the End of the Century: One Hundred Years of Architecture.* (New York: Abrams, 1998.)

Forty, Adrian. *Words and Buildings: A Vocabulary of Modern Architecture.* (London: Thames & Hudson, 2000.)

Levine, Neil. *Modern Architecture: Representation & Reality.* (New Haven: Yale University Press, 2009).

Lucan, Jacques. *Composition, Non-Composition: Architecture and Theory in the Nineteenth and Twentieth Centuries.* (Abingdon: Routledge, 2012.)

Norberg-Schulz, Christian. *Principles of Modern Architecture.* (London: Andreas Papadakis, 2000.)

Sharp, Dennis and Catherine Cooke, eds. *The Modern Movement in Architecture: Selections from the Docomomo Registers.* (Rotterdam: 010 Publishers, 2000.)

Tournikiotis, Panayotis. *The Historiography of Modern Architecture.* (Cambridge, MA: MIT Press, 1999.)

Book series
—
'Modern Architectures in History' (London: Reaktion Books):
  Brazil (Richard J. Williams, 2009);
  Britain (Alan Powers, 2007);
  Finland (Roger Connah, 2005);
  France (Jean-Louis Cohen, 2015);
  Greece (Alexander Tzonis & Alcestis P. Rodi, 2013);
  India (Peter Scriver & Amit Srivastava, 2015);
  Italy (Diane Yvonne Ghirardo, 2012);
  Russia (Richard Anderson, 2015);
  Turkey (Sibel Bozdogan & Esra Akcan, 2012);
  USA (Gwendolen Wright, 2008).

Reference works
—
Olmo, Carlo Maria, ed. *Dizionario dell'architettura dell XX secolo* in six volumes. (Torino: Umberto Allemandi & Co., 2000.)

Conrads, Ulrich, ed., Tr. by Michael Bullock. *Programs and Manifestos on 20th-Century Architecture.* (Cambridge, MA: MIT Press, 1970.)

Ockman, Joan and Edward Eigen. *Architecture Culture, 1943–1968: A Documentary Anthology.* (New York: Rizzoli, 1993.)

Index

Figures in *italic* refer to illustrations

A

Aachen, Germany: St Fronleichnam (Schwarz) 48
Aalto, Alvar 207
  Baker House, MIT *114–15*
  Paimio Sanatorium 105
  Säynätsalo Town Hall *136*
  Villa Mairea *104, 116*
  Vyborg Library 82, *84*
Aarhus City Hall, Denmark (Jacobsen and Møller) *109*
ABK: Cummins Engine Factory, Glasgow *235*
Acceptera (Modernist manifesto) 82
AEG Turbine Factory, Berlin (Behrens) *21*
Ahmedabad: Indian Institute of Management, Vastrapur (L. Kahn) *221*
Ahrends, Peter *see* ABK
Airstream 'Clipper' Caravan (Byam) *166*
Albert, Prince: Victoria and Albert Museum of Childhood, Bethnal Green, London *11*
Alexander, Christopher: Houses of Mexicali, Mexico *200*
Alfeld an der Leine, Germany: Fagus Factory (Gropius and Meyer) 13, *22*
Algiers: El Madania district (Pouillon) *141*
Alsop, Will 251, 262
  see also Alsop & Störmer
Alsop & Störmer: Hôtel du Département des Bouches du Rhône, Marseilles *262*
American Bar, Kärnter Durchgang, Vienna (Loos) *19*
American Folk Art Museum, New York (Williams Tsien Architects) *279*
Amsterdam
  Borneo Sporenburg Housing (West 8) *266*
  Eigen Haard Housing (de Klerk and Kramer) *57*
  Municipal Orphanage (van Eyck) *154*
  Solid 11, Constantijn Huygenstraat (Fretton) *290*
  Stock Exchange (Berlage) *16*
Ando, Tadao: 21_21 Design Sight, Tokyo *223*
Antoniuskirche, Basel (Moser) *47*
Anttinen, Selina *see* AOA
AOA (Anttinen, Selina and Oiva, Vesa): Helsinki University Main Library *288*
Apeldoorn, Netherlands: Centraal Beheer (Hertzberger) 161, *178*
Appia, Adolphe 35
Arau, Higini 279
Archigram group 256
Architects Co Partnership: Margaret Wix Primary School *170*
Architectural Association, London 251
Architecture Studio: Institut du Monde Arabe (with Nouvel) *240–41*

'Architecture without Architects'
(exhibition, 1964) 122
Arkan, Seyfi: Atatürk's House, Istanbul 97
Arneberg, Arnstein, and Poulsson,
Magnus: Oslo City Hall 42
Arnos Grove Station, London (Holden) 51
Arnstein House (model), S_ Paulo
(Rudofsky) 122
art brut movement 125
Art Deco 20, 39
Art Nouveau 13, 23, 192
Arts & Architecture magazine 174
Arup, Ove 161, 176
Busaras, Dublin (canopy) 137
Spa Green Flats, Islington,
London 171
see also Koolhaas, Rem
Arup Associates (Dowson and Hobbs):
Mining and Metallurgy Building,
University of Birmingham 176
Asmara, Eritrea: Fiat Tagliero
Service Station (Pettazzi) 87, 97
Asplund, Erik Gunnar 105, 129
Gothenburg Law Courts 109, 110
Skandia Cinema, Stockholm 38
Stockholm Public Library 44
Woodland Cemetery, Stockholm 111
AT&T Building, New York (Johnson and
Burgee) 202
Atatürk, Mustafa Kemal 87
House, Istanbul (Arkan) 97
Atelier des Bâtisseurs (ATBAT): Unité
d'Habitation, Marseilles (with Le
Corbusier) 126
Atelier 5
St Bernard's, Croydon 154
Siedlung Halen, nr Berne 154
Atelier Soukup see Pawson, John
Ateliers Jean Nouvel: Cultural and
Congress Centre, Lucerne 254–55
Athens
Acropolis landscaping (Pikionis) 137
The Blue Building (Panyiotakos) 94
Aulenti, Gae: Musée d'Orsay, Paris
(conversion) 192
Austrian Postal Savings Bank, Vienna
(O. Wagner) 17

B
—
Badovici, Jean see Gray, Eileen
Bagsvaerd Church. nr Copenhagen
(Utzon) 207, 208–209
Bailey House (Case Study House No. 21),
Los Angeles (Koenig) 175
Baker House, MIT (Aalto) 114–15
Balfron Tower, Tower Hamlets, London
(Goldfinger) 140
Ban, Shigeru
cardboard cathedral 207
Christchurch Transitional Cathedral,
New Zealand 229
Japanese Pavilion, Hannover Expo
2000 229
Banfi, Gian Luigi, Barbaiano di Belgiojoso,
Ludovico, Peressutti, Ernico and
Rogers, Ernesto: Torre Velasca,
Milan 135
Bangalore: Academic Block of Indian
Institute of Management (Doshi)
207, 215
Banham, Peter Reyner 184
Barbaiano di Belgiojoso, Ludovico see
Banfi, Gian Luigi
Barcelona
Casa Bloc Housing, Sant Andreu
(Sert, Clavé and Subirana) 89

Colònia Güell Chapel crypt (Gaudí) 15
German Pavilion, International
Exposition (1929; Mies van der
Rohe) 7
National Theatre of Catalonia (Bofill
and Taller del Arquitectura)
204–205
Barceloneta: Apartments, Calle Bach
(Coderch) 138
Bardi, Lina Bo: SESC Leisure Centre,
São Paulo 207, 212
Barozzi, Pabrizio see Estudio Barozzi Veiga
Barragán, Luis: La Fuente de los Amantes,
Los Clubes, Mexico 151
Barreca, Gianandrea see Boeri, Stefano
Bartoli, Giovanni see Nervi, Pier Luigi
Basel
Antoniuskirche (Moser) 47
Kollegienhaus, University of Basel
(Rohn) 106
Bauhaus 6, 48
Bauhaus building, Dessau (Gropius
and Meyer) 7, 71
BBC Arquitectos: Le Utthe Boutique,
La Plata 249
Beaudoin, Eugène and Lods, Marcel
Cité de la Muette, Drancy 170
Maison du Peuple, Paris 165
BedZED, Hackbridge, Surrey (Dunster/
ZEDfactory) 231, 245
Beek, Paul van see West 8
Bègles, France: Centre de Soins de
Jour (Lacaton & Vassal) 276
Behnisch, Günther see Otto, Frei
Behrens, Peter 13
AEG Turbine Factory, Berlin 21
Beijing
National ('Bird's Nest') Stadium
(Herzog and de Meuron) 251
Women's Dormitory (Liang and Lin)
100
Bellot, Dom. Paul: Quarr Abbey, Isle
of Wight 27
Benscheidt, Karl 22
Bentley, John Francis: Westminster
Cathedral, London 24–25
Bergen, Norway: Villa Konow (Lund) 112
Bergsten, Carl 9
Stadsteatern, Götaplatsen,
Gothenburg 9
Berkel, Ben van see UNStudio
Berkeley, California: First Church
of Christ Scientist (Maybeck) 27
Berlage, Hendrik Petrus 13
Amsterdam Stock Exchange 16
Berlin
AEG Turbine Factory (Behrens) 21
Friedrichstrasse Skyscraper (Mies
van der Rohe) 60
Hufeisensiedlung, Britz (Taut,
M. Wagner and Migge) 72
Jewish Museum (Libeskind) 251, 253
Philharmonie (Scharoun) 145
Social housing, Kreuzberg (Krier)
200–201
Bernofsky, Gene and Jo Ann, Kallweit,
Richard and Richert, Clark: Drop
City, Trinidad, Colorado 161, 167
béton brut 125, 127
Bexhill on Sea, East Sussex: De La
Warr Pavilion (Mendelsohn and
Chermayeff) 118
Bijvoet, Bernard see Chareau, Pierre
Bilbao, Spain: Guggenheim Museum
(Gehry) 251, 252, 260
Binswanger, Christine see Herzog
& de Meuron

Biosphere, Montreal (Fuller) 163
Birmingham, University of: Mining
and Metallurgy Building (Arup
Associates) 176
Bizley, Graham see Prewett Bizley
Architects
Blaisse, Petra 258
Bloomfield Hills, Michigan: Cranbrook
Academy of Art (Eliel Saarinen)
58–59
Bo, Jørgen see Wohlert, Vilhelm
Bodiansky, Vladimir
Maison du Peuple, Paris 165
Unité d'Habitation, Marseilles 126
Boeri, Stefano: Bosco Verticale, Milan
(with Barreca and La Varra) 231, 246
Bofill, Ricardo and Taller del Arquitectura:
National Theatre of Catalonia,
Barcelona 204–205
Böhm, Dominikus 48
St Kamillus, Mönchengladbach 47
Bonatz, Paul
Stuttgart Hauptbahnhof (with
Scholer) 50
Town Hall Watertower,
Kornwestheim 108
Boodles House, Liverpool (Jiřičná) 243
Booth, George G. 59
Borbiró, Virgil and Králik, László: Budaörs
Airport, Budapest 88
Bordeaux
Centre de Soins de Jour, Bègles
(Lacaton & Vassal) 275, 276
Faculté de Médecine et de Pharmacie
(Pascal) 31
Bos, Caroline see UNStudio
Bosco Verticale, Milan (Boeri, Barreca
and La Varra) 231, 246
Boston, Massachusetts
Hancock Tower (Cobb) 142
Quincy Market Development
(Thompson and Associates) 188
Botta, Mario: Church of St John the
Baptist, Mogno, Switzerland 220
Bourdelle, Antoine 23
Boyarsky, Alvin 251
Boyd, Robin 102
Brandhorst Museum, Munich
(Sauerbruch Hutton) 261
Brangwyn, Frank 55
Brasilia: National Congress (Niemeyer)
132
Breuer, Marcel 103
UNESCO House, Paris (with Nervi
and Zehrfuss) 133
see also Roth, Alfred and Emil
Brinkman, Johannes and Vlugt, Leendert
van der: Van Nelle Factory,
Rotterdam 66, 68–69
Brion Cemetery extension, Treviso
(Scarpa) 207, 211
Brno, Moravia
Crematorium Chapel (Wiesner) 49
Villa Tugendhat (Mies van der Rohe
and Reich) 76
Brooks, Van Wyck 39
Brussels: Palais Stoclet (Hoffmann) 20
Brutalism 125, 127
Bryggman, Erik: Resurrection Chapel
117
Budapest: Budaörs Airport (Borbiró and
Králik) 88
Bunshaft, Gordon see Skidmore, Owings
and Merrill
Burgee, John see Johnson, Philip
Burnham, Daniel: Civic Center,
Chicago (proposed) 36

BuroHappold see Cullinan, Edward
Burton, Richard see ABK
Busaras, Store Street, Dublin (Scott) 137
Byam, Wallace ('Wally'): Airstream
'Clipper' Caravan 166
Byron, Robert 30

C
—
Cage, John 167
Calatrava, Santiago: Gare de Saint
Exupéry, Lyons 236–37
California Case Study Houses 161, 175,
232
California School System Design
(Ehrenkrantz) 232
Cambridge, England: Schlumberger
Gould Research Centre (Hopkins
Architects) 242
Cambridge, Massachusetts: 9 Ash Street
(Johnson) 144
Cantacuzino, George Matei: Hotel Belona,
Eforie Nord, Romania 92–93
Caribbean Hut (Semper) 10
Caruso (Adam) and St John (Peter)
Architects
New Art Gallery, Walsall 275, 277
Stotorget repaving scheme, Kalmar,
Sweden 274
Victoria and Albert Museum of
Childhood, Bethnal Green,
London 11
Carver Court, Coatesville, Penn. (Howe,
Stonorov and L. Kahn) 123
Cascais, Portugal: Casa das Histórias
Paula Rego (Souto de Moura) 219
Case Study Houses see California Case
Study Houses
Castanheira, Carlos see Siza Vieira,
Álvaro
Centraal Beheer, Apeldoorn, The
Netherlands (Hertzberger) 161, 178
Centre Pompidou, Paris (Piano and
Rogers) 231, 234–35
Chace House, West Hollywood
(Schindler) 164
Chambellan, Rene: Daily News Building
sculpture 53
Chandigarh, India: The High Court
(Corbusier and Pierre Jeanneret) 127
Chareau, Pierre and Bijvoet, Bernard:
Maison de Verre, Paris 75
Chermayeff, Serge see Mendelsohn, Erich
Chicago
Civic Center (Burnham; proposed) 36
Tribune Tower (Howells and Hood)
53, 59
World's Columbian Exposition (1893)
36
Childs, David: One World Trade Center,
New York 272
China Academy of Art Conference Centre,
Hangzhou (Kuma) 284
Chipperfield, David: The Hepworth,
Wakefield 275, 283
Christchurch Transitional Cathedral,
New Zealand (Ban) 229
Church of the Sky, Jeju, South Korea
(Itami Jun Architects) 275, 282
CIAM (Congrès International
d'Architecture Moderne) 47, 72,
88, 94, 125, 188
Cité de la Muette, Drancy (Beaudoin
and Lods) 170
'Ciudad Lineal, La' (Soria y Mata) 32
Clavé, Josep Torres see Sert, Josep Lluís
Clos Pegase Winery, Napa Valley,

California (Graves) 189

Coatesville, Penn.: Carver Court (Howe, Stonorov and L. Kahn) 123

Cobb, Henry N.: Hancock Tower, Boston 142

Coderch i de Sentmenat, José Angonio: Apartments, Calle Bach, Barceloneta 138

Cologne: Theatre, Deutscher Werkbund Exhibition (van de Velde) 23

Colònia Güell Chapel, Barcelona (Gaudí) 15

Commerzbank Tower, Frankfurt (Foster + Partners) 239, 244

Como, Italy: Casa del Fascio (Terragni) 65, 81

Constructivism, Russian 63

Cook, Peter and Fournier, Colin: Kunsthaus Graz 257

Cooke, Bernard Stanley see Martienssen, Rex

Copenhagen: Klampenborg petrol station (Jacobsen) 89

Corbusier, Le (Charles Jeanneret) 94, 102, 105, 125, 137, 161, 215
High Court, Chandigargh (with Pierre Jeanneret) 127
Notre Dame du Haut, Ronchamp 125, 128, 264
Roq et Rob Housing Project, Roquebrune-Cap-Martin 124, 154
Unité d'Habitation, Marseilles 126
Villa Savoye, Poissy (with Pierre Jeanneret) 7, 74
Villa Stein De Monzie, Vaucresson/ Garches (with Pierre Jeanneret) 74

Cork Institute of Technology: Student Centre Building (De Blacam & Meagher) 286-87

Correa, Charles
Kanchanjunga Apartments, Mumbai 215
Navi Mumbai 214

Coruña, La, Spain: Domus, Museum of Mankind (Isosaki) 216

Cram, Ralph Adams: Cathedral of St John the Divine, New York 26

Cranbrook Academy of Art, Michigan (Eliel Saarinen) 58-59

Cret, Paul Philippe 39
Mastbaum Foundation, Rodin Museum Philadelphia (with Gréber) 45

Croydon, Surrey: St Bernard's (Atelier 5) 154

Cruz, Marco da see Sjölander da Cruz Architects

Culbert, Tim see SANAA

Cullinan, Edward, and Partners (with BuroHappold): Weald and Downland Museum, West Sussex 207, 224-25

Cummins Engine Factory, Glasgow (ABK) 235

Cusato, Marianne: Katrina Cottage 228

Cuypers, Pierre 57

Czech Pavilion, Exposition Internationale...dans la Vie Moderne, Paris (1937) (Krejcar) 86

D
—

Daem, Hilde see Robbrecht & Daem

Dalcroze Institute Festspielhaus, Gartenstadt Hellerau, Dresden (Tessenow) 35

Dattner Architects and Grimshaw Architcts: Via Verde, Bronx, New York 246

De Blacam (Shane) & Meagher (John): Student Centre Building, Cork Institute of Technology 286-87

De Carlo, Giancarlo: Il Magistero, Urbino University 153

Deconstructivism 252

Decq, Odile see Studio Odile Decq

Degania Kibbutz School, Israel (Kauffmann) 96

Delhi, New
US Embassy (Stone) 185
Viceroy's House (Lutyens) 30

Dessau, Germany: Bauhaus (Gropius and Meyer) 7, 71

Deutscher Werkbund 73
exhibition (Cologne, 1914) 23

Dixon (Jeremy) Jones (Edward) Architects: Royal Opera House extension, Covent Garden, London 9

Domus, Museum of Mankind, La Coruña (Isosaki) 216

Dong Nai, Vietnam: Farming Kindergarten (Vo Trong Nghia) 294-95

Doshi, Balkrishna Vithaldas 220
Academic Block of Indian Institute of Management, Bangalore 207, 215

Downland Gridshell see Weald and Downland Museum

Dowson, Sir Philip see Arup Associates

Dresden: Dalcroze Institute Festspielhaus, Gartenstadt Hellerau (Tessenow) 35

Drop City, Trinidad, Colorado (G. and J. Bernofsky, Kallweit and Richert) 161, 167

Duany, Andrés 228

Dublin: Busaras, Store Street (Scott) 137

Dudok, Willem Marinus: Hilversum Town Hall 41

Duiker, Johannes (Jan): Zonnestraal Sanatorium, Hilversum 66-67

Dundon Passivhaus, Somerset (Prewett Bizley Architects) 8

Dunican, Peter see Lubetkin, Berthold

Dunster, Bill 231, 247
see also Dunster Architects

Dunster Architects/ZEDfactory: BedZED, Hackbridge, Surrey 231, 245

Dushkin, Alexey: Novoslobodskaya Metro Station, Moscow 50

Düsseldorf: Nordrhein Westfalen Museum (unbuilt; Stirling and Wilford) 182

Dykers, Craig Edward see Snøhetta

Dymaxion House (Fuller) 161, 162

E
—

Eames, Charles and Ray: Eames House 232

Edinburgh: Scottish Parliament Building (Miralles and Tagliabue) 207, 226-27

Eforie Nord, Romania: Hotel Belona (Cantacuzino) 92-93

Ehrenkrantz, Ezra: California School System Design 232

Eisenman, Peter 251
Wexner Center for the Arts, Ohio State University 252

Emerson, Ralph Waldo 105

Entenza, John 174

Epstein, Jacob 277

Eriksson, Nils Einar: concert hall, Gothenburg 9

Erith, Raymond: Frog Meadow, Dedham, Essex 184

Erskine, Ralph
Byker Wall Estate, Newcastle upon Tyne (with Gracie) 213
housing, Gyttorp, Sweden 136

Esprit Nouveau, L' 61

Estudio Barozzi Veiga: Filharmonia, Szczecin 279

Ettedgui, Joseph 242

Évora, Portugal: Quinta da Malagueira (Siza Vieira) 218

Eyck, Aldo van 178
Municipal Orphanage, Amsterdam 154

F
—

Faaborg Museum, Denmark (Petersen) 45

Fagus Factory, Alfeld an der Leine (Gropius and Meyer) 13, 22

Fallingwater, Pennsylvania (Wright) 105, 105, 120

Fan Wenzhao (Robert Fan): Majestic Theatre staircase, Shanghai 101

Farkasréti Cemetery Chapel (Makowecz) 217

Farming Kindergarten, Vietnam (Vo Trong Nghia) 294-95

Fassler, John see Martienssen, Rex

FAT (Fashion Architecture Taste): New Islington, Manchester 268-69

Fathy, Hassan 199

Fehn, Sverre 207
Hedmark Museum, Hamar, Norway 210

Ferraz, Marcelo 212

Fiat Lingotto Works, Turin (Trucco) 61, 78-79

Fiat Tagliero Service Station, Asmara (Pettazzi) 87, 97

Filharmonia, Szczecin (Estudio Barozzi Veiga) 279

Finlay, Ian Hamilton: Garden Temple, Dunsyre, Scotland 194

First Church of Christ Scientist. Berkeley, California (Maybeck) 27

Fischer, Theodor 96
7-10 Lechfeldstrasse, Munich Laim 35

Florence: Santa Maria Novella Station (Michelucci and Gruppo Toscano) 80

Florence, Alabama: Rosenbaum House (Wright) 164

Foreign Office Architects: Yokohama Ferry Terminal 264

Foster, Norman 231, 231, 232
see also Foster + Partners

Foster + Partners
Commerzbank Tower, Frankfurt 239, 244
Swiss Re (The Gherkin), London 273
Willis Faber Dumas Offices, Ipswich 230, 233, 242

Fournier, Colin see Cook, Peter

Franco, General Francisco 89, 138

Frank, Josef 103
installation drawing 107

Frankfurt am Main
Commerzbank Tower (Foster + Partners) 239, 244
Museum of Decorative Arts (Meier) 194-95
Siedlung Römerstadt (May) 61, 73

Fretton, Tony: Solid 11, Constantijn Huygenstraat, Amsterdam 290

Frog Meadow, Dedham, Essex (Erith) 184

Fuchs, Bohuslav: Zelená Žaba (Green Frog) Pool Complex, Slovakia 90

Fuksas, Doriana and Massimiliano: Mainz Market House 270-71

Fuller, Richard Buckminster 161, 167
Biosphere, Montreal 163
Dymaxion House 161, 162
geodesic domes 161, 163
Wichita House 160

Futurism 13 61, 79

Futuro House (Suuronen) 181

G
—

Games, Abram: Your Britain... (poster) 119

Garatti, Vittorio: School of Music, Havana 214

Gardella, Ignazio: House on the Zattere, Venice 183, 184

'Garden City' plan (Howard) 34

Garden Temple, Dunsyre, Scotland (Finlay) 194

GATCPAC collective 87, 89

Gatwick Airport (Hoar, Marlow and Lovett) 88

Gaudí, Antoni 226
Colònia Güell Chapel, Barcelona 15

GEHAG 72

Gehry, Frank 251
Guggenheim Museum, Bilbao 251, 252, 260

Genoa: Grattacielo Martini (Piacentini and Invernizzi) 54

geodesic domes (Fuller) 161, 163

German Pavilion, International Exposition, Barcelona (1929) (Mies van der Rohe) 7

Geuze, Adriaan see West 8

Ghent: Market Hall (Robbrecht & Daem) 275, 290

Giedion, Sigfried 6, 77
Building in France, Building in Iron 6

Gigliotti, Vittorio: Mosque of Rome, Parioli, Rome 198

Gilbert, Cass: Woolworth Building, New York 37

Gill, Irving 164

Ginsburg, Mosei and Milinis, Ignati: Narkomfin Communal House, Moscow 64

Glancey, Jonathan 217

Glasgow School of Art (Mackintosh) 14

Goetz Collection, Munich (Herzog & de Meuron) 276

Golden Gate Exhibition (1939) 107

Goldfinger, Ernö: Balfron Tower, Tower Hamlets 140

Golosov, Ilya 63
Zuev Workers' Club, Moscow 65

Goodhue, Bertram Grosvenor: Nebraska State Capitol, Lincoln 43

Goodwin, Philip see Stone, Edward Durrell

Gotardi, Roberto: School of Theatre, Havana 214

Gothenburg, Sweden
Law Courts (Asplund) 109, 110
Stadsteatern (Bergsten) 9

Gowan, James see Stirling, James

Gracie, Vernon see Erskine, Ralph

Graves, Michael 194
Clos Pegase Winery, California 189

Gray, Eileen: Villa E 1027, Roquebrune Cap Martin (with Badovici) 75

Graz, Austria: Kunsthaus (Cook and Fournier) 257

Gréber, Jacques see Cret, Paul

Griffiths, Sean see FAT
Grimshaw, Nicholas 231
Grimshaw Architects see Dattner
    Architects
Groningen, The Netherlands: La Liberté
    Housing (Perrault) 267
Gropius, Walter 13, 103, 152, 161, 178
    Bauhaus, Dessau (with Meyer) 7, 71
    Fagus Factory, Alfeld an der Leine
        (with Meyer) 13, 22
Grounds, Roy 102
Gruppo Toscano see Michelucci, Giovanni
Guggenheim Museum, Bilbao (Gehry) 251,
    252, 260
Guggenheim Museum, New York (Wright)
    131
Gyttorp, Sweden: housing (Erskine) 136

H
—
Habitat 67, Montreal (Safdie) 4, 161, 172–73
Hadid, Zaha 251, 251
    MAXXI, Rome 260, 261
Hagen, Ole: Villa, Liseleje, Denmark 8
Haifa, Israel: Municipal Hospital
    (Mendelsohn) 119
Halprin, Lawrence: Promontory Point, Sea
    Ranch, California 186
Hannover Expo 2000
    Japanese Pavilion (Ban) 229
    Netherlands Pavilion (MVRDV) 265
Harrison, Wallace K. see Hood, Raymond
Haslemere: Olivetti Training Centre
    (Stirling) 180
Havana, Cuba: National Art Schools
    (Gottardi, Porro and Garatti) 214
Havlíček, Josef and Honzík, Karel:
    General Pension Institute, Prague 88
Havre, Le, France (reconstruction)
    (Perret) 56
Hedmark Museum, Hamar, Norway
    (Fehn) 210
Hee, Marie José van see Robbrecht
    & Daem
Heidegger, Martin 207
Heins, George Lewis: Cathedral of St
    John the Divine, New York (with
    LaFarge) 26
Helsingborg, Sweden: Concert Hall
    (Markelius) 82–83
Helsinki
    Central Railway Station (Eliel
        Saarinen) 28–29
    University Main Library (AOA) 288
Hepworth, The, Wakefield (Chipperfield)
    275, 283
Herrmann & Steinberg Hat Factory,
    Luckenwalde (Mendelsohn) 70
Hertzberger, Herman: Centraal Beheer,
    Apeldoorn 161, 178
Herzog (Jacques) & de Meuron (Pierre)
    Goetz Collection, Munich 276
    National ('Bird's Nest') Stadium,
        Beijing 251
    New North Zealand Hospital,
        Denmark 231, 249
Hill, Oliver 111
Hilversum, Netherlands
    Town Hall (Dudok) 41
    Zonnestraal Sanatorium (Duiker)
        66–67
Hitchcock, Henry Russell 7, 105
Hoar, Marlow and Lovett: Gatwick
    Airport 88
Hobbs, Ronald see Arup Associates
Hoffmann, Josef: Palais Stoclet,
    Brussels 20

Holden, Charles: Arnos Grove Station,
    London 51
Holl, Steven: Chapel of St Ignatius, Seattle
    University 264
Holland, Charles see FAT
Hollein, Hans: Schullin Jewellery Shop II,
    Vienna 188
Honzík, Karel see Havlíček, Josef
Hood, Raymond
    Daily New Building, New York
        (with Howells) 53
    RCA Building, New York (with
        Harrison) 55
Hopkins Architects (Michael and Patricia
    Hopkins) 231
    Kroon Hall School of Forestry, Yale
        University (with Centerbrook
        Architects) 247
    Schlumberger Gould Research
        Centre, Cambridge 242
Horiguchi, Sutemi: Wasaka House,
    Tokyo 100
Howard, Ebenezer: 'Garden City' plan 34
Howe, George, Stonorov, Oscar and Kahn,
    Louis: Carver Court, Coatesville,
    Penn. 123
Howells, John Mead and Hood, Raymond
    Daily News Building, New York 53
    Tribune Tower, Chicago 53
Hruška, Emanuel 95
Humlebaek, Denmark: Louisiana Museum
    (Wohlert and Bo) 149
Hutton, Louisa see Sauerbruch Hutton

I
—
Imrey Culbert (Celia Imrey and Tim
    Culbert) see SANAA
INA Building, EUR, Rome (Muzio,
    Paniconi and Pediconi) 52
Ingierstrand Baths, Oppegärd (Schistad
    and Moestue) 91
Intelace, Singapore (OMA) 275
International Style 7, 61, 105
Invernizzi, Angelo see Piacentini,
    Marcello
Isosaki, Arati: Domus, Museum of
    Mankind, La Coruña 216
Istanbul: Atatürk's House (Arkan) 97
Itami Jun Architects: Church of the Sky,
    Jeju, South Korea 275, 282
Ito, Toyo: Sendai Mediatheque, Japan 256

J
—
Jacob, Sam see FAT
Jacobsen, Arne
    Aarhus City Hall (with Møller) 109
    Klampenborg petrol station,
        Copenhagen 89
Jacoby, Helmut 231
Jeanneret, Pierre see Corbusier, Le
Jeddah: Corniche Mosque (El Wakil) 199
Jeju, South Korea: Church of the Sky
    (Itami Jun Architects) 275, 282
Jencks, Charles 183, 188
Jewish Museum, Berlin (Libeskind) 251,
    253
Jiřičná, Eva 231
    Boodles House, Liverpool 243
Johannesburg: Stern House (Martienssen,
    Fassler & Cooke) 102
Johansen, John: Mummers Theater,
    Oklahoma City 161, 178
Johnson, Philip 7, 183
    9 Ash Street, Cambridge, Mass. 174
    AT&T Building, New York (with

Burgee) 202
    see also Mies van der Rohe, Ludwig
Johnson Wax Building, Racine, Wisconsin
    (Wright) 121
Jones, Edward see Dixon Jones Architects
Jong, Wessel de 66
Jugendstil 47
Jun Itami see Itami Jun Architects

K
—
Kahn, Ely Jacques 103
Kahn, Louis 45, 151, 215, 287
    Indian Institute of Management,
        Ahmedabad, India 221
    Kimbell Art Museum, Fort Worth,
        Texas 190
    'The Room' 206
    Yale University Art Gallery 148–49
    see also Howe, George
Kalmar, Sweden: repaving scheme
    (Caruso St John) 274
Karajan, Herbert von 145
Katrina Cottage (Cusato) 228
Kauffmann, Richard: Degania Kibbutz
    School, Israel 96
Kelly, Michael see De Blacam & Meagher
Kempsey Museum and Visitor Centre,
    NSW (Murcutt) 207, 224
Kenwood, House, Nairobi (May) 98
Kimbell Art Museum, Fort Worth, Texas
    (L. Kahn) 190
Klerk, Michel de and Kramer, Piet:
    'The Ship', Eigen Haard Housing,
    Amsterdam 57
Klimt, Gustav 20
Klint, Kaare 45
Kochi University of Technology (Kikumi
    Watanabe): School Floating in the
    Sky, Thailand 275, 291
Koenig, Pierre: Bailey House (Case Study
    House No. 21), Los Angeles 175
Kokoschka, Oskar 19
Koolhaas, Rem 251, 251
    Casa da Música, Porto (with OMA
        and Arup) 258
Koralek, Paul see ABK
Korin, Pavel 50
Kornwestheim, Germany: Town Hall
    Watertower (Bonatz) 108
Korsmo, Arne: Villa Stenersen, Oslo 113
Králik, László see Borbíró, Virgil
Kramer, Piet see Klerk, Michel de
Krejcar, Jaromir
    Czech Pavilion, Exposition
        Internationale..., Paris (1937) 86
    Sanatorium Machnáč, Slovakia 90
Krier, Léon 200
Krier, Rob: Social housing, Berlin 200–201
Kroll, Lucien: Maison Médicale, Louvain
    University 207, 212
Kuma, Kengo: Academy of Art Conference
    Centre, Hangzhou 284
Kunsthaus Graz, Austria (Cook and
    Fournier) 257
Kurokawa, Kisho: Nagakin Capsule
    Tower Hotel, Tokyo 161, 179

L
—
Lacaton (Anne) & Vassal (Jean Philippe):
    Centre de Soins de Jour, Bègles,
    France 275, 276
Lafarge, Christopher Grant see Heins,
    George Lewis
Lambert, Phyllis 130
Larkin Building, Buffalo (Wright) 121

Lasdun, Denys: Royal College of
    Physicians, London 150–51
Lauritzen, Vilhelm see Herzog & de
    Meuron
La Varra, Giovanni see Boeri, Stefano
Leadenhall Building ('The Cheesegrater'),
    London (Rogers Stirk Harbour) 273
Leicester Engineering Building (Stirling
    and Gowan) 125, 156
Lens, France: Louvre outstation (SANAA)
    275
Levitt, Alfred and William: Levittown,
    Long Island, New York 166
Lewerentz, Sigurd: St Peter's, Skåne 129
Liang Sicheng and Lin Huiyin: Women's
    Dormitory, Beijing 100
Libeskind, Daniel 251
    Chamber Works 250
    Jewish Museum, Berlin 251, 253
    World Trade Center, New York 272
Lille: Tour Crédit Lyonnais (Portzamparc)
    263
Lin Huiyin see Liang Sicheng
Lincoln, Nebraska: State Capitol
    (Goodhue) 43
Lisbon: National Mint (Segurado and
    Varela) 96
Liseleje, Denmark: Villa (Hagen) 8
Löbau, Germany: Schminke House
    (Sharoun) 77
Lods, Marcel see Beaudoin, Eugène
Löfdahl, Eva 275
London
    Arnos Grove Station (Holden) 51
    Balfron Tower, Tower Hamlets
        (Goldfinger) 140
    Economist Buildings (A. and P.
        Smithson) 157
    Finsbury Helth Centre (Lubetkin
        and Tecton) 119
    Leadenhall Building ('The
        Cheesegrater') (Rogers Stirk
        Harbour) 273
    London School of Economics Student
        Centre, London (O'Donnell &
        Tuomey) 275, 289
    Royal College of Physicians (Lasdun)
        150–51
    Royal Festival Hall (LCC, Matthew,
        Martin and Moro) 134
    Royal Opera House extension (Dixon
        Jones Architects) 9
    Segal Close and Walters Way,
        Lewisham (Segal) 167
    Spa Green Flats, Islington (Lubetkin
        and Tecton) 171
    Swiss Re ('The Gherkin') (Foster)
        273
    Victoria and Albert Museum of
        Childhood (Prince Albert) 11
    Westminster Cathedral (Bentley)
        24–25
Loos, Adolf 85, 290
    American Bar, Kärnter Durchgang,
        Vienna 19
    Tribune Tower, Chicago (competition
        entry) 53
Los Angeles
    Bailey House (Case Study House
        No. 21) (Koenig) 175
    Lovell Health House (Neutra) 85
    Star Apartments (Maltzan) 275, 291
Los Clubes, Mexico: La Fuente de los
    Amantes (Barragán) 151
Louisiana Museum, Humlebaek, Denmark
    (Wohlert and Bo) 149
Louvain University: Maison Médicale

(Kroll) 207, *212*
Lovell Health House, Los Angeles
(Neutra) *85*
Lubetkin, Berthold and Tecton
Finsbury Health Centre, London *119*
Spa Green Flats, Islington, London
(with Arup and Dunican) *171*
Lucerne: Cultural and Congress Centre
(Ateliers Jean Nouvel) *254–55*
Luckenwalde, Germany: Herrmann &
Steinberg Hat Factory (Mendelsohn)
70
Lugano: Library (C. and R. Tami) *107*
Lund, Frederik Konow: Villa Konow,
Bergen *112*
Lundqvist, John: sculpture *111*
Lutyens, Sir Edwin: Viceroy's House,
New Delhi *30*
Lyndon, Donlyn see MLTW
Lynn, Jack see Womersley, J. Lewis
Lyon: Gare de Saint Exupéry (Calatrava)
236–37
Lyotard, Jean François 183

M
—
Maas, Winy see MVRDV
Mackintosh, Charles Rennie 20, 226,
293
Glasgow School of Art *14*
Mainz Market House, Germany (M. and D.
Fuksas) *270–71*
Maison de Verre, Paris (Chareau and
Bijvoet) *75*, 231
Maison du Peuple, Paris (Beaudoin and
Lods) *165*, 231
Makowecz, Imre: Farkasréti Cemetery
Chapel *217*
Maltzan, Michael: Star Apartments, LA
275, *291*
Manchester: New Islington (FAT) *268–69*
Manship, Paul: *Prometheus* 55
Marbach, Stefan see Herzog & de Meuron
Markelius, Sven: Concert Hall,
Helsingborg *82–83*
Marseilles
Hôtel du Département des Bouches
du Rhône (Alsop & Störmer) *262*
Unité d'Habitation (Corbusier) *126*
Martienssen, Rex, Fassler, John and
Cooke, Bernard Stanley: Stern House,
Johannesburg *102*
Martin, Leslie see Matthew, Robert
Massachusetts Institute of Technology
(MIT): Baker House (Aalto) *114–15*
Matthew, Robert, Martin, Leslie and
Moro, Peter: Royal Festival Hall,
London *134*
MAXXI, Rome (Hadid) 260, *261*
May, Ernst
Kenwood House, Nairobi *98*
Siedlung Römerstadt, Frankfurt
61, *73*
Maybeck, Bernard: First Church of Christ
Scientist, Berkeley, California *27*
Meagher, John see De Blacam & Meagher
Meier, Richard: Museum of Decorative
Arts, Frankfurt *194–95*
Melbourne: Stanhill (Romberg) *102*
Melnikov, Konstantin: Rusakov Workers'
Club, Moscow *62–63*
Mendelsohn, Erich 85
De La Warr Pavilion, Bexhill (with
Chermayeff) *118*
Haifa Municipal Hospital *119*
Herrmann & Steinberg Hat Factory,
Luckenwalde *70*

Mergenthaler, Ascan see Herzog & de
Meuron
Mérida, Spain: Museo Nacional de Arte
Romano (Moneo) *193*
Mesiniaga Tower, Selangor (Yeang) *244*
Metabolist movement 158, 179
Mexicali Houses, Mexico (Alexander) *200*
Meyer, Adolf see Gropius, Walter
Michelucci, Giovanni and Gruppo
Toscano: Santa Mara Novella
Station, Florence *80*
Mies van der Rohe, Ludwig 48, 61, 125,
188, 275
Apartment House,
Weissenhofsiedlung, Stuttgart *73*
Friedrichstrasse Skyscraper,
Berlin *60*
German Pavilion, Barcelona
Exposition (1929) *7*
Seagram Building, New York (with
Johnson) *130*
Villa Tugendhat, Brno (with Reich) *76*
Migge, Leberecht see Taut, Bruno
Milan
Bosco Verticale (Boeri, Barreca and
La Varra) 231, *246*
Church of San Francesco al
Fopponino (Ponti) *139*
Torre Velasco (Banfi, Barbaiano di
Belgiojoso, Peressutti and
Rogers) *135*
Milinis, Ignati see Ginsburg, Mosei
Milles, Carl: sculpture *58–59*
Miralles, Enric: Scottish Parliament
Building, Edinburgh (with Tagliabue)
207, *226–27*
MIT see Massachusetts Institute
of Technology
Mitterrand, François 251, 262
MLTW (Moore, Lyndon, Turnbull and
Whitaker): Promontory Point, Sea
Ranch, California *186*
Mockbee, Samuel see Rural Studio
Modena, Italy: San Cataldo Cemetery
(Rossi) *196–97*
'Modern Architecture: International
Exhibition', Museum of Modern Art,
New York 7, *7*, 174
Modernism 6–7, 9, 10, 39, 87, 105, 183,
275, 279
Moestue, Eyvind see Schistad, Ole Lind
Mogno, Switzerland: Church of St John
the Baptist (Botta) *220*
Moholy Nagy, László: book cover design *6*
Møller, see Jacobsen, Arne
Mönchengladbach, Germany: St Kamillus
(Böhm) *47*
Moneo, Rafael: Museo Nacional de Arte
Romano, Mérida, Spain *193*
Montreal
Biosphere (Fuller) *163*
Habitat 67 (Safdie) *4*, 161, *172–73*
Montuori, Eugenio and Vitellozzi,
Annibale: Stazione Termini, Rome
133
Moore, Charles 183, 186
see also MLTW
Moore, Henry: sculpture *133*
Mopin, Eugène: Cité de la Muette *170*
Moro, Peter see Matthew, Robert
Mosbach, Catherine see SANAA
Moscow
Metro *39*
Mostorg Department Store (Vesnin
brothers) *65*
Narkomfin Communal House
(Ginsburg and Milinis) *64*

Novoslobodskaya Metro Station
(Dushkin) *50*
Rusakov Workers' Club (Melnikov)
62–63
Zuev Workers' Club (Golosov) *65*
Moser, Karl: Antoniuskirche, Basel *47*
Mousawi, Sami: Mosque of Rome, Parioli,
Rome *198*
Moussavi, Farshid see Foreign Office
Architects
Muji see Ryohin, Mujirushi
Mumbai: Kanchanjunga Apartments
(Correa) *215*
Mummers Theater, Oklahoma City
(Johansen) 161, *178*
Munich
Brandhorst Museum (Sauerbruch
Hutton) *261*
Olympic Stadium (Otto and
Behnisch) *177*
Munich Laim: 7–10 Lechfeldstrasse
(Fischer) *35*
Murcutt, Glen: Kempsey Museum and
Visitor Centre, NSW 207, *224*
Musée d'Orsay, Paris (conversion;
Aulenti) *192*
Mussolini, Benito 54, 81
Mujirushi Ryohin: The Urban House *245*
Muzio, Giovanni, Paniconi, Mario and
Pediconi, Giulio: INA Building, EUR,
Rome *52*
MVRDV (Maas, van Rijs and de Vries):
Netherlands Pavilion, Hannover
Expo 2000 *265*

N
—
Nagakin Capsule Tower Hotel, Tokyo
(Kurosawa) 161, *179*
Nairobi: Kenwood House (May) *98*
Nanjing, China: Great Relic Museum
(Studio Odile Decq) *261*
Navi Mumbai (Correa) *214*
Nebraska State Capitol, Lincoln
(Goodhue) *201*
Nervi, Pier Luigi 161
Air Force Hangar, Orvieto (with
Bartoli) *176*
see also Breuer, Marcel
Neutra, Richard 174
Lovell Health House, Los Angeles *85*
New Brutalism 157
New Building (*Neues Bauen*) 61
'New City' project (Sant'Elia) *12*
New North Zealand hospital, Denmark
(Herzog & Meuron) *231*
New Objectivity (*Neue Sachlichkeit*) 61
New York
American Folk Art Museum
(Williams Tsien Architects) *279*
AT&T Building (Johnson and
Burgee) *202*
Cathedral of St John the Divine
(Heins, LaFarge and Cram) *26*
Daily News Building (Howells and
Hood) *53*
Guggenheim Museum (Wright) *131*
Levittown, Long Island (A. and W.
Levitt) *166*
'Modern Architecture: International
Exhibition' (1932) 7, *7*
Museum of Modern Art (Stone and
Goodwin) *185*
RCA Building (Hood and Harrison) *55*
Seagram Building (Mies van der
Rohe and Johnson) *130*
TWA Flight Center, JFK Airport

(Eero Saarinen) *143*
Via Verde, Bronx (Dattner and
Grimshaw) *246*
Woolworth Building (Gilbert) *37*
World Trade Center (Childs) *272*
World's Fair (1939) *107*
'New York Five' 194
Newcastle upon Tyne: Byker Wall Estate
(Erskine and Gracie) *213*
Niemeyer, Oscar
Church of St Francis of Assisi,
Pampulha *132*
National Congress, Brasilia *132*
Nishizawa, Ryue see SANAA
Nissen, Peter Norman: Nissen Hut *162*
Noero, Jo see Noero Wolff Architects
Noero Wolff Architects: Red Location
Museum, Port Elizabeth, South
Africa *226*
Noormarkku, Finland: Villa Mairea
(Aalto) *104*, 116
Norberg Schulz, Christian 420
Nouvel, Jean
Institut du Monde Arabe, Paris
240–41
see also Ateliers Jean Nouvel

O
—
Oak Park, Illinois: Unity Temple
(Wright) *18*
O'Donnell (Sheila) & Tuomey (John):
Student Centre, LSE 275, *289*
Ohio State University: Wexner Center
for the Arts (Eisenman) *252*
Oiva, Vesa see AOA
Okabe, Noriaki see Piano, Renzo
Oklahoma City: Mummers Theater
(Johansen) 161, *178*
OMA (Office of Metropolitan Architecture)
260
The Interlace, Singapore (with RSP
Architects) 275, *288*
see also Koolhaas, Rem
Oppegärd, Norway: Ingierstrand Baths
(Schistad and Moestue) *91*
Orvieto: Air Force Hangar (Nervi and
Bartoli) *176*
Oslo
City Hall (Arneberg and Poulsson) *42*
Norwegian National Opera and
Ballet (Snøhetta) 275, *280–81*
Villa Stenersen (Korsmo) *113*
Östberg, Ragnar: Stockholm City Hall *40*
Otto, Frei 161
Munich Olympic Stadium (with
Behnisch) *177*
Oud, Jacobus Johannes Pieter
Kiefhoek Housing Estate,
Rotterdam *72*

P
—
Pacific Science Center, Seattle
(Yamasaki) *152*
Paimio Sanatorium, Finland (Aalto) *105*
Palais Stoclet, Brussels (Hoffmann) *20*
Pamphulha: Church of St Francis
(Niemeyer) *132*
Paniconi, Mario see Muzio, Giovanni
Panyiotakos, Kyriakos: The Blue Building,
Athens *94*
Paris
Apartments, 26 rue Vavin (Sauvage
and Sarazin) *33*
Centre Pompidou (Piano and Rogers)
231, *234–35*

Exposition Internationale... (1937) *86*
Institut du Monde Arabe (Architecture Studio and Nouvel) *240–41*
Maison de Verre (Chareau and Bijvoet) *75*, 231
Maison du Peuple (Beaudoin and Lods) *165*, 231
Musée d'Orsay (conversion; Aulenti) *192*
National Musée des Travaux Publics (Palais d'Iéna) (Perret) *44*
Notre Dame du Raincy (Perret) *47*
Prefabricated Housing, Meudon (J. and H. Prouvé, and Sive) *168–69*
Théâtre des Champs Élysées (Perret) *23*
UNESCO House (Breuer, Nervi and Zehrfuss) *133*
Pärnu, Estonia: Beach Pavilion (Siinmaa) *89*
Parris, Alexander: Quincy Market, Boston *188*
Pascal, Jean Louis: Faculté de Médecine et de Pharmacie, Bordeaux *31*
Pawley, Martin 143
Pawson, John, and Atelier Soukup: Abbey of Our Lady of Nový Dvur, Bohemia *278*
Pedicone, Giulio *see* Muzio, Giovanni
Pei, Ioeh Ming 142
Pennsylvania, University of: Clinical Research Building (Venturi and Scott Brown) *203*
Peressutti, Enrico *see* Banfi, Gian Luigi
Perrault, Dominique: La Liberté Housing, Groningen *267*
Perret, Auguste 13, 39, 140
Le Havre, France (reconstruction) *56*
National Musée des Travaux Publics (Palais d'Iéna), Paris *44*
Notre Dame du Raincy, Paris *47*
Théâtre des Champs Élysées, Paris *23*
Petersen, Carl: Faaborg Museum, Denmark *45*
Pettazzi, Giuseppe: Fiat Tagliero Service Station, Asmara *87*, *97*
Philadelphia, Penn.: Mastbaum Foundation, Rodin Museum (Cret and Gréber) *45*
Piacentini, Marcello and Invernizzi, Angelo: Grattacielo Martini, Genoa *54*
Piano, Renzo
Pompidou Centre, Paris (with Rogers) 231, *234–35*
Terminal One, Kansai Airport, Osaka (with Okabe) *238–39*
Pick, Frank 51
Pikionis, Dimitris: Acropolis landscaping *137*
Plata, La, Argentina: Le Utthe Boutique (BBC Arquitectos) *249*
Platz, Gustav Adolf 65, 79
Plečnik, Jože: Church of the Most Sacred Heart of Our Lord, Prague *46*
Plischke, Ernst: Kahn House, Wellington *103*
Poelzig, Hans 97
Pompidou Centre, Paris (Piano and Rogers) 231, *234–35*
Ponti, Giò: Church of San Francesco al Fopponino, Milan *139*
Porro, Ricardo: School of Plastic Arts, Havana *214*
Port Elizabeth, South Africa: Red Location

Museum (Noero Wolff Architects) *226*
Port Grimaud, Var, France (Spoerry) *183*, *187*
Porto, Portugal: Casa da Música (Koolhaas, OMA and Arup) *258*
Portoghesi, Paolo: Mosque of Rome, Parioli, Rome *198*
Portzamparc, Christian de: Tour Crédit Lyonnais *263*
Postmodernism 10, 183, 189, 203, 207, 269
Potsdam, Germany: Einstein Tower (Mendelsohn) *71*
Pouillon, Fernand 140
El Madania district, Algiers *141*
Poulsson, Magnus *see* Arneberg, Arnstein
Pound, Ezra 183
Prague
Church of the Most Sacred Heart of Our Lord (Plečnik) *46*
General Pension Institute (Havlíček and Honzík) *88*
Schnirchova Apartment Block (Rosenberg) *95*
Prairie Houses (Wright) 40
Prewett (Robert) Bizley (Graham) Architects: Dundon Passivhaus, Somerset *8*
Promontory Point, Sea Ranch, California (Halprin and MLTW) *186*
Prouvé, Henri *see* Prouvé, Jean
Prouvé, Jean 161, 165, 170
Maison du Peuple, Paris *165*, 231
Prefabricated Housing, Meudon, Paris (with H. Prouvé and Sive) *168–69*

Q
—
Quarr Abbey, Isle of Wight (Bellot) *27*
Quincy Market Development, Boston, Mass. (Thompson and Associates) *188*

R
—
Racine, Wisconsin: Johnson Wax Administration Building (Wright) *121*
Rauschenberg, Robert 167
Red Location Museum, Port Elizabeth, South Africa (Noero Wolff Architects) *226*
Rego, Paula 219
Reich, Lilly *see* Mies van der Rohe, Ludwig
Resurrection Chapel, Turku (Bryggman) *117*
Rice, Peter
aerofoil roof 239
Centre Pompidou, Paris *234–35*
Richardson, H. H. 29
Rijs, Jacob van *see* MVRDV
Robbrecht (Paul) & Daem (Hilde), with van Hee, Marie José: Market Hall, Ghent 275, *290*
Roche, Kevin 235
Rockefeller, John D. 55
Villa E 1027 (Gray and Badovici) *75*
Rogers, Ernesto Nathan *see* Banfi, Gian Luigi
Rogers, Richard 231, 232, 233
see also Rogers Stirk Harbour
Rogers Stirk Harbour: The Leadenhall Building, London *273*
Rohn, Roland: Kollegienhaus, University of Basel *106*
Romberg, Frederick: Stanhill, Melbourne

102
Rome
INA Building, EUR (Muzio, Paniconi and Pediconi) *52*
MAXXI (Hadid) *260*, 261
Mosque of Rome, Parioli (Portoghesi) *198*
Stazione Termini (Gruppo Montuori and Gruppo Vitellozzi) *133*
Ronchamp, France: Notre Dame du Haut (Corbusier) 125, 128, *264*
'Room, The' (L. Kahn) *206*
Roquebrune Cap Martin: Roq et Rob Housing Project (Corbusier) *124*, 154
Rosenberg, Eugene: Schnirchova Apartment Block, Prague *95*
Rossi, Aldo 183
San Cataldo Cemetery, Modena *196–97*
Roth, Alfred and Emil, and Breuer, Marcel: Doldertal Apartments, Zurich *76*
Rotterdam
Kiefhoek Housing Estate (Oud) *72*
Van Nelle Factory (Brinkman and van der Vlugt) 66, *68–69*
Rouse, James 188
Royal College of Physicians, London (Lasdun) *150–51*
Royal Festival Hall, London (LCC, Matthew, Martin and Moro) *134*
Royal Opera House extension, Covent Garden, London (Dixon Jones Architects) *9*
RSP Architects: The Interlace, Singapore (with OMA) 275, *288*
Rudofsky, Bernard: Arnstein House, São Paulo (model) *122*
Rudolph, Paul 120
Art and Architecture Building, Yale University *152*
Ruppin, Arthur 96
Rural Studio
Hale County works 207
$20K House, Alabama *228*
Ruth, D. K. *see* Rural Studio

S
—
Saarinen, Eero 59, 144, 232, 235, 247
TWA Flight Center, JFK Airport, New York *143*
Saarinen, Eliel 143
Helsinki Central Railway Station *28–29*
Tribune Tower, Chicago (competition entry) 53, 59
Safdie, Moshe: Habitat 67, Montreal 4, 161, *172–73*
St Albans: Margaret Wix Primary School (Architects Co Partnership) *170*
St John, Peter *see* Caruso St John
Salvisberg, Otto 102
SANAA: Louvre Lens, Lens, France 275, *285*
Sant'Elia, Antonio: The 'New City' project *12*
São Paolo: SESC Leisure Centre (Bardi) 207, *212*
Sarazin, Charles *see* Sauvage, Henri
Sau, Luke Him: Bank of China, Shanghai *99*
Sauerbruch, Matthias *see* Sauerbruch Hutton
Sauerbruch Hutton: Brandhorst Museum, Munich *261*
Sauvage, Henri, and Sarazin, Charles:

Apartments, 26 rue Vavin, Paris *33*
Säynätsalo, Finland: Town Hall (Aalto) *136*
Scarpa, Carlo 183
Brion Cemetery extension, Treviso 207, *211*
Museo Civico di Castelvecchio, Verona (conversion) *190*
Scharoun, Hans
Berlin Philharmonie *145*
Schminke House, Löbau *77*
Scheeren, Ole *see* OMA
Schindler, Rudolf 85
Chace House, West Hollywood *164*
Schistad, Ole Lind and Mostue, Eyvind: Ingierstrand Baths, Oppegård, Norway *91*
Schminke House, Löbau (Scharoun) *77*
Scholer, Firedrich Eugen *see* Bonatz, Paul
School Floating in the Sky, Thailand (Kochi University of Technology) *275*, *291*
Schütte Lihotzky, Margarete: kitchens 73
Schwarz, Rudolf: St Fronleichnam, Aachen *48*
Scott, Michael: Busaras, Dublin *137*
Scott Brown, Denise *see* Venturi, Robert
Scottish Parliament Building, Edinburgh (Miralles and Tagliabue) 207, *226–27*
Seagram Building, New York (Mies van der Rohe and Johnson) *130*
Seattle, Washington
Chapel of St Ignatius, Seattle University (Holl) *264*
Pacific Science Center (Yamasaki) *152*
Segal, Walter: Segal Close and Walters Way, Lewisham, London *167*
Segurado, Jorge de Almeida and Varela, Antonio: National Mint, Lisbon *96*
Seidler, Harry: Rose Seidler House, Sydney *103*
Sejima, Kazuyo *see* SANAA
Selangor: Mesiniaga Tower (Yeang) *244*
Semper, Gottfried 16, 47, 275
Caribbean Hut *10*
Sendai Mediatheque, Japan (Ito) *256*
Sert, José Maria 55
Sert, Josep Lluís, Clavé, Josep Torres and Subirna, Joan Baptista: Casa Bloc Housing, Sant Andreu, Barcelona *89*
SESC Leisure Centre, S_o Paulo (Bardi) 207, *212*
Shanghai
Bank of China (Sau) *99*
Majestic Theatre staircase (Fan) *101*
Sheffield: Park Hill Flats (Womersley, Lynn and I. Smith) *155*
Siedlung Halen, nr Berne (Atelier 5) *154*
Siinmaa, Olev: Beach Pavilion, Pärnu, Estonia *89*
Singapore: Interlace (OMA) 275
Siza Vieira, Álvaro
Chemical Plant Offices, Jiangsu Province. China (with Castanheira) 275, *292–93*
Quinta da Malagueira, Évora, Portugal *218*
Sjölander, Maria *see* Sjölander da Cruz Architects
Sjölander da Cruz Architects: River Studio, Leaminton Spa 231, *248*
Skåne, Sweden: St Peter's (Lewerentz) *129*

Skidmore, Owings and Merrill/Bunshaft: Beineke Library, Yale University 146–47, 152
see also Childs, David
Smith, George Kidder 106, 133
Smith, Ivor see Womersley, J. Lewis
Smithson, Alison and Peter 9, 187
Economist Buildings, London 157
Snøhetta (Dykers and Thorsen): Norwegian National Opera and Ballet, Oslo 275, 280–81
Sochi, Russia: Sanatorium (Stschussew) 65
Solid 11, Constantijn Huygenstraat, Amsterdam (Fretton) 290
Sony Tower, New York see AT&T Building
Soria y Mata, Arturo: 'La Ciudad Lineal' 32
Souto da Moura, Eduardo: Casa das Histórias Paula Rego, Cascais, Portugal 219
Spoerry, François: Port Grimaud, Var, France 183, 187
Stadsteatern, Götaplatsen, Gothenburg (Bergsten) 9
Stalin, Josef/Stalinism 10, 39, 87
Stirk, Graham see Rogers Stirk Harbour
Stirling, James 9, 183
Leicester Engineering Building (with Gowan) 125, 156
Neue Staatsgalerie, Stuttgart (with Wilford) 191
Nordrhein Westfalen Museum, Düsseldorf (with Wilford) 182
Olivetti Training Centre, Haslemere 180
Stockholm
City Hall (Östberg) 40, 50
Public Library (Asplund) 44
Skandia Cinema (Asplund) 38
Woodland Cemetery (Asplund) 111
Stone, Edward Durrell
Museum of Modern Art, New York (with Goodwin) 185
US Embassy, New Delhi 185
Stonorov, Oscar see Howe, George
Störmer, Jan see Alsop & Störmer
Strnad, Oskar 103
Stschussew, A.: Sanatorium, Sochi 65
Studio Odile Decq: Great Relic Museum 261
Stuttgart 74
Apartment House, Weissenhofsiedlung (Mies van der Rohe) 73
Hauptbahnhof (Bonatz and Scholer) 50
Mercedes Benz Museum (UNStudio) 259
Neue Staatsgalerie (with Wilford) 191
Subirana, Joan Baptista see Sert, Josep Lluís
Sullivan, Louis 19, 37
Suuronen, Matti: Futuro House 181
Svenkst Tenn (company) 107
Swiss Re ('The Gherkin'), London (Foster) 273
Sydney
Opera House (Utzon) 144, 251
Rose Seidler House (Seidler) 103

T
—
Tagliabue, Benedetta see Miralles, Enric
Taller del Arquitectura see Bofill, Ricardo
Tami, Carlo and Rino: Library, Lugano 107
Tange, Kenzō 216
Yoyogi National Gymnasium, Tokyo

158–59
Taut, Bruno: Hufeisensiedlung, Britz (with M. Wagner and Migge) 72
Team 10 125, 157
Tecton see Lubetkin, Berthold
Teige, Karel 90
Terragni, Giuseppe: Casa del Fascio 65, 81
Terry, Quinlan 184
Tessenow, Heinrich: Dalcroze Institute Festspielhaus, Garten Hellerau, Dresden 35
Thompson (Benjamin) and Associates: Quincy Market Development, Boston, Mass. 188
Thorsen, Kjetil Traedl see Snøhetta
'Ticino School' 220
Tokyo
Nagakin Capsule Tower Hotel (Kurosawa) 161, 179
21_21 Design Sight (Ando) 223
Wasaka House (Horiguchi) 100
Yoyogi National Gymnasium (Tange) 158–59
Trenčianske Teplice, Slovakia
Sanatorium Machnáč (Krejcar) 90
Zelená Žaba (Green Frog) Pool Complex (Fuchs) 90
Trucco, Giacomo Matté: Fiat Lingotto Works, Turin 61, 78–79
Tsien, Billie see Williams Tsien Architects
Tuomey, John see O'Donnell, Sheila
Turin: Fiat Lingotto Works (Trucco) 61, 78–79
Turku, Finland: Resurrection Chapel (Bryggman) 117
Turnbull, William see MLTW
$20K House, Alabama (Rural Studio) 228
21_21 Design Sight, Tokyo (Ando) 223

U
—
Unité d'Habitation, Marseilles (Corbusier) 126
United States Embassy, New Delhi (Stone) 185
Unity Temple, Oak Park, Illinois (Wright) 18
UNStudio: Mercedes Benz Museum, Stuttgart 259
Urban House, The (Mujirushi Ryohin) 245
Urbino University: Il Magistero (De Carlo) 153
Utthe Boutique, Le, La Plata (BBC Arquitectos) 249
Utzon, Jørn 207
Bagsvaerd Church, nr Copenhagen 207, 208–209
Sydney Opera House 144, 251

V
—
Vals, Switzerland: Thermal Baths (Zumthor) 207, 222
Varela, Antonio see Segurado, Jorge de Almeida
Vassal, Jean Philippe see Lacaton & Vassal
Vaucresson/Garches, France: Villa Stein De Monzie (Corbusier and Pierre Jeanneret) 74
Veiga, Alberto see Estudio Barozzi Veiga
Velde, Henry van de: Theatre, Deutscher Werkbund Exhibition 23
Venturi, Robert 183, 202
Clinical Research Building, University of Pennsylvania

(with Scott Brown) 203
Verona: Museo Civico di Castelvecchio (conversion) (Scarpa) 190
Vesnin, Alexander, Leonid and Viktor: Mostorg Department Store, Moscow 65
Viceroy's House, New Delhi (Lutyens) 30
Victoria and Albert Museum of Childhood, Bethnal Green, London (Prince Albert; extension, Caruso St John Architects) 11
Vienna
American Bar, Kärnter Durchgang (Loos) 19
Austrian Postal Savings Bank (O. Wagner) 17
Schullin Jewellery Shop II (Hollein) 188
Villa, Liseleje, Denmark (Hagen) 8
Villa E 1027, Roquebrune Cap Martin (Gray and Badovici) 75
Villa Konow, Bergen (Lund) 112
Villa Mairea, Finland (Aalto) 104, 116
Villa Savoye, Poissy, France (Corbusier and Pierre Jeanneret) 7, 7, 74
Villa Stein De Monzie, Vaucresson/ Garches (Corbusier and Pierre Jeanneret) 74
Villa Stenersen, Oslo (Korsmo) 113
Villa Tugendhat, Brno (Mies van der Rohe and Reich) 76
Viollet le Duc, Eugène 16
Vitellozzi, Annibale: Stazione Termini, Rome 133
VKhUTEMAS School, Moscow 63
Vlugt, Leendert van der see Brinkman, Johannes
Vo Trong Nghia Architects: Farming Kindergarten, Vietnam 294–95
Vries, Nathalie de see MVRDV
Vyborg, Russia: Library (Aalto) 82, 84

W
—
Wagner, Martin see Taut, Bruno
Wagner, Otto 13, 47
Austrian Postal Savings Bank, Vienna 17
Wakefield: The Hepworth (Chipperfield) 275, 283
El-Wakil, Abdel Wahid: Corniche Mosque, Jeddah 199
Walsall: New Art Gallery (Caruso St John) 275, 277
Wang Shu 284
Watanabe, Kikumi see Kochi University of Technology
Weald and Downland Museum, West Sussex (Cullinan with BuroHappold) 207, 224–25
Wellington, New Zealand: Kahn House (Plischke) 103
West 8: Borneo Sporenburg Housing, Amsterdam 266
Westminster Cathedral, London (Bentley) 24–25
Whitaker, Richard see MLTW
Wichita House (Fuller) 160
Wiesner, Arnošt: Crematorium Chapel, Brno 49
Wilford, Michael see Stirling, James
Williams, Tod see Williams Tsien Architects
Williams Tsien Archtects: American Folk Art Museum, NYC 279
Willis Faber Dumas Offices, Ipswich (Foster + Partners) 230, 233, 242

(with Scott Brown) 203

Wogenscky, André: Unité d'Habitation, Marseilles 126
Wohlert, Vilhelm and Bo, Jørgen: Louisiana Museum, Humlebaek, Denmark 149
Wolfe, Tom 185
Wolff, Heinrich see Noero Wolff Architects
Wölfflin, Heinrich 6
Womersley, J. Lewis, Lynn, Jack, and Smith Ivor: Park Hill Flats, Sheffield 155
Woolworth Building, New York (Gilbert) 37
World Trade Center, New York (Childs) 272
Wright, Frank Lloyd 13, 103, 105, 125, 164, 293
Fallingwater, Bear Run, Penn. 105, 105, 120
Johnson Wax Administration Building 121
Larkin Building, Buffalo 121
Prairie Houses 40
Rosenbaum House, Florence, Alabama 164
Unity Temple, Oak Park, Illinois 18
Wurster, William 115

Y
—
Yale University, New Haven, Conn.
Art and Architecture Building (Rudolph) 152
Art Gallery (Kahn) 148–49, 190
Beineke Library (Skidmore, Owings and Merrill/Bunshaft) 46–47, 152
Kroon Hall School of Forestry (Hopkins Architects and Centerbrook Architects) 247
Yamasaki, Minoru 272
Pacific Science Center, Seattle 152
Yeang, Ken 231
Mesiniaga Tower, Selangor 244
Yokohama Ferry Terminal, Japan (Foreign Office Architects) 264
Yorke Rosenberg Mardall 95
Yoyogi National Gymnasium, Tokyo (Tange) 158–59

Z
—
Zaera Polo, Alejandro see Foreign Office Architects
Zattere, The, Venice: House (Gardella) 183, 184
Zehrfuss, Bernard see Breuer, Marcel
Zelená Zaba (Green Frog) Pool Complex, Slovakia (Fuchs) 90
Zenghelis, Elia 258
Zumthor, Peter: Thermal Baths, Vals, Switzerland 207, 222
Zurich: Doldertal Apartments (A. and E. Roth and Breuer) 76

Picture Credits

The author and publisher would like to thank the following companies and individuals for permission to reproduce images in this book. In all cases, every effort has been made to credit the copyright holders, but should there be any omissions or errors the publisher would be pleased to insert the appropriate acknowledgement in any subsequent edition of this book.

T = top
B = bottom
L = left
R = right

Frontispiece: Stéphane Groleau/Alamy
6 Private collection, London
7 The Museum of Modern Art Archives, IN15.1.© 2015. Digital image, The Museum of Modern Art, New York/Scala, Florence
8T Private collection, London
8B Image courtesy Graham Bizley
9T Alan Powers
9B Image courtesy Dixon Jones Ltd.
10 Private collection, London
11 Hélène Binet
12 RIBA Collections
14 John Peter Photography/Alamy
15 age fotostock/Alamy
16 Image courtesy Beurs van Berlage
17 Angelo Hornak/Alamy
18 B.O'Kane/Alamy. © ARS, NY and DACS, London 2015
19 Hemis/Alamy
20 Angelo Hornak/Alamy
21 INTERFOTO/Alamy
22 Novarc Images/Alamy
23L Private collection, London
23R "Theatre des Champs Elysees" © Auguste PERRET, UFSE, SAIF, 2015 and DACS
24 A.P.S. (UK)/Alamy
26 Heritage Image Partnership Ltd/Alamy
27T Image courtesy Daniella Thompson
27B John Henshall/Alamy
28 Ian Shaw/Alamy
30 Chris Hellier/Alamy
31 © ROUSSEL IMAGES/Alamy
32 Private collection, London
33 Hemis/Alamy
34 Private collection, London
35T Kunstbibliothek, Staatliche Museen zu Berlin. Inventory No:. KBB 9925 © 2015. Photo Scala, Florence/bpk, Bildagentur fuer Kunst, Kultur und Geschichte, Berlin
35B Wikimedia/Peterf/CC-BY-SA-3.0
36 Library of Congress
37 GL Archive/Alamy
38 Courtesy Arkdes, Stockholm
40 Anna Idestam-Almquist/Alamy
41 Arcaid Images/Alamy
42 Universal Images Group/DeAgostini/Alamy
43 Sunpix Travel/Alamy
44T © Collection Artedia/View Pictures

Ltd. "Palais d'Iéna" Auguste PERRET, UFSE, SAIF, 2015 and DACS
44B Robert Matton AB/Alamy
45T Courtesy of the Philadelphia Museum of Fine Art
45B Hélène Binet
46 isifa Image Service s.r.o./Alamy
47T Wikimedia/Ikiwaner/CC-BY-SA-3.0
47B Photo courtesy and © Gisbert Fongern
48 Bildarchiv Monheim GmbH/Alamy
49 Wikimedia/Michal Klajban/Podzemnik/CC-BY-SA-3.0
50T © Hulton-Deutsch Collection/Corbis
50B Barry Lewis/Alamy
51 VIEW Pictures Ltd/Alamy
52 Lautaro/Alamy
53 AA World Travel Library/Alamy
54 Adam Eastland/Alamy
55 © Swim Ink 2, LLC/Corbis
56 Hemis/Alamy
57 Arcaid Images/Alamy
58 © Stephen Saks Photography/Alamy
60 Friedrichstrasse Skyscraper, project. Berlin-Mitte, Germany, 1921. Perspective of north-east corner. New York, Museum of Modern Art (MoMA). Charcoal and graphite on brown paper, mounted on board, 68 ¼ x 48' (173.4 x 121.9 cm). The Mies van der Rohe Archive. Gift of the architect. Acc. n.: 1005.1965. © 2015. Digital image, The Museum of Modern Art, New York/Scala, Florence. © DACS 2015
61, 64 Richard Pare
65T, 65C Private collection, London
65B Richard Pare
66, 68 Alan Powers
70 Bildarchiv Monheim GmbH/Alamy
71 imageBROKER/Alamy
72T Private collection, London
72B, 73L Bildarchiv Monheim GmbH/Alamy
73R Alan Powers
74T © FLC/ADAGP, Paris and DACS, London 2015
74B VPC Travel Photo/Alamy © FLC/ADAGP, Paris and DACS, London 2015
75T RIBA Library Photographic Collection
75B Photo courtesy and © Mark Lyon
76T Unidentified photographer. Marcel Breuer papers, Archives of American Art, Smithsonian Insitution (Image no. 1019)
76B isifa Image Service s.r.o./Alamy. © DACS 2015
77 Eva Gruendemann/Alamy
78 Paul Raftery/Alamy
80 picturesbyrob/Alamy
81 imageBROKER/Alamy
82 Alan Powers
84 Museum of Finnish Architecture
85 © G.E. Kidder Smith/Corbis
86 Prague National Technical Museum/AKG-images
88T Wikimedia/trepex
88B Private collection, Germany
89T Photo: Martin Siplane/Museum of Estonian Architecture
89B, 90T Private collection, London
90B Photo: Archive of the Department of Architecture at USTARCH SAV
91 Jim Heimann Collection/Getty Images
92 Private collection, London
94 photo Benaki Museum, Neohellenic

Architecture Archives
95 Architectural Press Archives/RIBA Collections
96T Library of Congress
96B Wikipedia/Manuelvbotelho
97T Wikimedia/Stambouliote
97B Eric Lafforgue/Alamy
98 Eckhard Ferrel, Frankfurt/Main (Ernst-May-Gesellschaft)
99 from: Modernism in China by Edward Denison
100T Art, Architecture and Engineering Library, University of Michigan
100B, 101 from: Modernism in China by Edward Denison
102T Photo by Wolfgang Sievers, State Library, Victoria, Australia
102B RIBA Collections
103T National Library of New Zealand, Te Puna Mātauranga o Aotearoa, Alexander Turnbull Library, Irene Koppel Collection Reference: 35mm-35607-5-F Photograph by Irene Koppel
103B Danielle Tinero/RIBA Collections
104 Alvar Aalto Museum
106 G.E. Kidder Smith
107T Image courtesy of Svenskt Tenn Archive, Stockholm
107B Prisma Bildagentur AG/Alamy
108 Photo: Rose Hajdu
109 © Nikreates/Alamy
110 Peter Blundell-Jones
111 Arcaid Images/Alamy
112, 113 Jiri Havran
114 Arcaid Images/Alamy
116 Museum of Finnish Architecture
117 Courtesy Ola Laiho
118 Alan Powers
119T Estate of Abram Games
119B RIBA Collections
120 National Geographic Image Collection/Alamy
121 © John Ferro Sims/Alamy. © ARS, NY and DACS, London 2015
122 Bernard Rudofsky, Model for Arnstein House, Sao Paolo, 1939–41, Photo Sochi Sunami, Research Library, The Getty Institute, Los Angeles/© DACS 2015
123 Louis I. Kahn Collection, University of Pennsylvania and the Pennsylvania Historical and Museum Commission. Photo by Gottscho-Schleisner.
124 © FLC/ADAGP, Paris and DACS, London 2015
126 Sarah Franklin Photography/Stockimo/Alamy. © FLC/ ADAGP, Paris and DACS, London 2015
127 Galit Seligmann/Alamy. © FLC/ADAGP, Paris and DACS, London 2015
128 David Reed/Alamy. © FLC/ ADAGP, Paris and DACS, London 2015
129 Alan Powers
130 Mathias Beinling/Alamy
131T imageBROKER/Alamy. © ARS, NY and DACS, London 2015
131B Dorling Kindersley Ltd/Alamy
132T Keystone Pictures USA/Alamy
132B Steve Outram/Alamy
133T Angelo Hornak/Alamy
133B Adam Eastland/Alamy
134 Alan Powers
135 M.Flynn/Alamy
136T Museum of Finnish Architecture;

136B Wikipedia/Bengt Oberger
137T Architectural Press Archive/RIBA Collections
137B Hélène Binet
138 Rosmi Duaso/Alamy
139 Arcaid Images/Alamy
140 A.P.S. (UK)/Alamy
141 Thierry Grun/Alamy
142 Philip Scalia/Alamy
143 Arcaid Images/Alamy
144 Doug Steley A/Alamy
145 LOOK Die Bildagentur der Fotografen GmbH/Alamy
146 Michael Doolittle/Alamy
148 Bernard O'Kane/Alamy
149 John Woods/Alamy
150 Arcaid Images/Alamy
151 Wikimedia/Susleriel. © 2015 Barragan Foundation/DACS
152T www.paulrudolph.org
152B Ron Buskirk/Alamy Stock Photo
153 Fulvio Palma, Urbino
154T Aldo Van Eyck Archive
154B ETH Bibliothek, Zurich
155 Martin Pick/Alamy
156 Arcaid Images/Alamy
157 © Nigel Green
158 Moonie's World/Alamy
160, 162T Courtesy, The Estate of R. Buckminster Fuller
162B Private collection, London
163 © Tracey Whitefoot/Alamy
164T Photo © Grant Mudford
164B Arcaid Images/Alamy. © ARS, NY and DACS, London 2015
165 Alan Powers. © ADAGP, Paris and DACS, London 2015
166T Everett Collection Historical/Alamy
166B Shockpix Select/Alamy
167L Walter Segal Self Build Trust
167R Carl Iwasaki/The Life Images Collection/Getty Images
168 Alan Powers. © ADAGP, Paris and DACS, London 2015
170T Private collection, Paris
170B Alan Powers
171 Used with permission. John Murray Press/Hodder & Stoughton Ltd
172 Stéphane Groleau/Alamy
174 Cambridge Historical Commission
175 Arcaid Images/Alamy
176T CSAC Università di Parma/Sezione Fotografia/Fondo Vasari
176B Courtesy Arup Associates
177 Pxel / Alamy
178T Image by Herman Herzberger
178B Image courtesy of Mary Ann Sullivan
179 Islemount Images/Alamy
180 Richard Einzig/arcaid.co.uk
181 RealyEasyStar/ Rodolfo Felici/Alamy
182 James Stirling/Michael Wilford Fonds/Collection Centre Canadien d'Architecture/Canadian Centre for Architecture, Montréal
184T Eamonn Canniffe
184B Alan Powers
185 © Corbis/Bettmann
186 Carol M. Highsmith Archive/Library of Congress
187 Peter Stone/Alamy
188T Philip Scalia/Alamy
188B Bildarchiv Monheim GmbH/Alamy
189 Patrick Batchelder/Alamy

190T Richard Bryant/Arcaid/Bridgeman Images
190B Ken Hurst/Stockimo/Alamy
191 Arcaid Images/Alamy
192 allOver images/Alamy
193 Bildarchiv Monheim GmbH/Alamy
194 By courtesy of the Estate of Ian Hamilton Finlay
195 Arcaid Images/Alamy
196 SFM ITALIA 2/Alamy
198 Stephen Bisgrove/Alamy
199 Copyright © 2013 Awwakil.com. All Rights Reserved
200T Image courtesy Christopher Alexander and the Center for Environmental Structure
200B Alan Powers
202 Arcaid Images/Alamy
203 B.O'Kane/Alamy
204 Stefano Politi Markovina/Alamy
206 Architecture Comes from the Making of a Room, 1971. Drawing for City/2 exhibition. Charcoal on tracing paper. Philadelphia Museum of Art, Gift of the Artist
208 FP Collection/Alamy
210 Alan Powers
211 Arcaid Images/Alamy
212T Courtesy Lucien Kroll
212B VIEW Pictures Ltd/Alamy
213 Washington Imaging/Alamy
214 Image courtesy John East
215L Charles Correa Associates
215R Photo: Sanyam Bahga
216 Sergio Azenha/Alamy
217 Photo by László György Sáros
218 VIEW Pictures Ltd/Alamy
219 © Bjanka Kadic/Alamy
220 ImageBROKER/Alamy
221 © VIEW Pictures Ltd/Alamy
222 Arcaid Images/Nicholas Kane/Alamy
223 Jeremy Sutton-Hibbert/Alamy
224L Iconsinternational.Com/Alamy
224R Arcaid Images/Alamy
226L Photo: Iwan Baan
226R David Cairns/Alamy
228T Photo: Josh Gibson
228B Courtesy and © Timothy Hursley
229 ScotStock/Alamy
230 © Helmut Jacoby/Foster + Partners
232T Ehrenkrantz Eckstut & Kuhn Architects
232B Photo by Julius Shulman/Library of Congress, Prints & Photographs Division, The Work of Charles and Ray Eames/© 2015 Eames Office, LLC (eamesoffice.com)
233 Arcaid Images/Alamy
234 Arcaid Images/Alamy
235 John Donat/RIBA Collections
236 Olivier Parent/Alamy. © DACS 2015
238, 239 Arcaid Images/Alamy
240 Photo: thomasmayerarchive.com/© ADAGP, Paris and DACS, London 2015
242 Neil Grant/Alamy
243 Arcaid Images/Alamy
244 B.O'Kane/Alamy
245T Alan Powers
245B Image courtesy of MUJI
246T Riccardo Sala/Alamy
246B © David Sundberg/Esto
247 Morley von Sternberg
248 Image courtesy: Kingspan Insulation
249T © 2015, Herzog & de Meuron, Basel
249B BBC, Bielsa , Breide, Ciarlotti Bidinost Arquitectos. (www.bbcarquitectos.com.ar) Photographer: Manuel Ciarlotti Bidinost (www.estudiohomeless.com)
250 Courtesy Studio Libeskind
252T Wikipedia/Joebengo
252B John Norman/Alamy
253 Prisma Archivo/Alamy
254 travelstock44/Alamy
256, 257 Arcaid Images/Alamy
258 © Hemis/Alamy. © OMA/DACS 2015
259 Petr Svarc/Alamy
260 Victor Finley-Brown/Alamy
261T Photo: Roland Halbe
261B imageBROKER/Alamy
262 Chris Hellier/Alamy
263 Bildarchiv Monheim GmbH/Alamy
264T View Pictures/Universal Images Group/Getty Images
264B B.O'Kane/Alamy
265 Arcaid Images/Alamy
266 Galit Seligmann/Alamy
267 Ger Bosma/Alamy
268 Lowefoto/Alamy
270 Arcaid Images/Alamy
272 Jack Aiello/Alamy
273 Justin Kase z12z/Alamy
274 Caruso St. John Architects
276T © Vincent Monthiers
276B © Nick Guttridge/View Pictures Ltd
277 Hélène Binet
278 image courtesy Jens Weber
279T © Chris Gascoigne/VIEW Pictures Ltd/Alamy
279B © Hufton+Crow/VIEW/Corbis
280 Alan Powers
282 Courtesy Sato Shinichi
283 Martin Priestley/Alamy
284 Edward Denison
285 Photo: Iwan Baan
286 © Peter Cook/View Pictures
288T Photo: Iwan Baan
288B © Mika Huisman
289 Jeffrey Blackler/Alamy
290L Image courtesy Tony Fretton Architects/Peter Cook
290R VIEW Pictures Ltd/Alamy
291T Photo: Iwan Baan
291B Image courtesy Kikuma Watanabe
292 FG + SG Architectural Photography
294 courtesy Gremsy
296 Riccardo Sala/Alamy

Acknowledgements

I am grateful to Philip Cooper at Laurence King for commissioning this book, to Alice Graham for her patient work as editor, to Angela Koo the copy editor, Liz Jones, proof reader, and John Dowling, designer, and to Peter Kent for the dogged pursuit of pictures and permissions. In the process of gathering pictures I have also called on the kindness of many friends – Peter Blundell-Jones, Eamonn Caniffe, John East, Elain Harwood and Marc Treib, in particular, and others whose names are acknowledged in the picture credits, also to Sandra Berghianou in Japan, Claudia Quiring at the DAM, Frankfurt, Dan Teodorovici in Stuttgart and Inez Zalduendo at Harvard for helping to bring some of the more elusive ones into the net.

304